YOUNG

RICH

&

SAVAGE

A STORY BY:

DEQUILLARAE

Published By: BIGGS PUBLISHING GROUP

YOUNG RICH & SAVAGE

Before they were rappers with national notoriety, before they were reality TV stars or known as "Mr. Frosty Blow" and "Smack Down," they knew each other as Juwan "Mr. Frosty Blow" King and Taelor "Smack Down" Peterson.

2002

CHAPTER 1:

OUTSIDE OF LANGLEY HIGH SCHOOL

PITTSBURGH, PENNSYLVANIA

Juwan King and one of his homies sat on his CLS, waiting for his little sister, "Money King," to get out of school.

"Aye, ain't you from Northview, yo?" Taelor Peterson asked.

"Why, lil nigga? What the fuck you askin' me questions fo'? I don't know you," Juwan King replied, coldly.

"I know that lil nigga. He from the Heights," Juwan's homie said.

"I never seen this lil nigga up that way," Juwan responded, looking Taelor up and down. He wore a velour Rocawear sweat suit, iced-out necklace, watch and bracelet.

"That's that bitch Chilli's son," Juwan's homie said, shaking his head up and down as if he was confirming the fact with himself.

"Oh, Chilli's ya moms?"

"Yea, she my ma. Hey, tho', I'm tryna get wit' you. I be seeing you doin' ya thing. I gotta couple dollars," Taelor informed Juwan.

"What's a couple dollars?" Juwan inquired, curious to find out what the young hustler was working with.

"'Bout fifteen stacks," Taelor told his small audience.

"Oh, yea? What you tryna do wit' that?" Juwan probed

"I was hopin' you could front me a bird, and I'll pay you the rest of the paper when I finish the work," Taelor returned.

"A bird, huh, lil nigga? Ha ha ha..." Juwan and his homie chuckled at the young hustler's ambition.

"Taelor, what you doin' talkin' to my brotha?" Money King walked up to the circle of hustlers.

"Oh, you know him, too, Money?" Juwan asked his little sister.

"Yea, his crazy butt is in my class, but he barely comes to school. He so caught up hustlin' like you," Money snarled with an expression of disgust on her face.

"Shut the fuck up, and get in the whip!" Juwan told Money. "You get in, too, youngin'. I'ma ride you over," he instructed Taelor, getting into his luxury car.

"He ain't ridin' wit' us!" Money sassed as she got in her brother's CLS.

"I said shut the fuck up, Money. Get in, lil homie," Juwan commanded Taelor.

After dropping his little sister off, Juwan drove Taelor to his house. "Yo, get that paper together. I'ma send my man back around wit' some'in' fo' you. How long you need to get it together?" Juwan quizzed.

"I already got it together."

"A'ight, cool. My man will be right back wit' that. Put ya number in his phone," Juwan muttered, passing Taelor his homie's phone.

Twenty minutes later, Juwan's homie pulled up in front of Taelor's house, and called him. "I'm out front," he told Taelor.

Rushing out of his house, Taelor got into Juwan's CLS, and passed Juwan's homie a plastic, white grocery bag with fifteen thousand dollars in it. "Here you go."

"This fifteen, right?"

"Yup. What's this?"

"A bird. You owe ten stacks."

"Okay, no problem."

****

Four months had passed before they knew it and the year was 2003. Taelor had been copping from Juwan for a few months. He had dropped out of school, but had advanced in his street education. He went from adding up numbers in a textbook to adding stacks of money up and weighing grams on a digital scale. From carrying books in a backpack to carrying bricks and guns in his backpack. From playing basketball in the school's gymnasium to balling on the streets. From jacking people for their Jay's to jacking hustlers for kilos.

By this time, Money had caught feelings for him, but Taelor was focused on getting his paper. At first, they were calling each other brother and sister, but Taelor started noticing how jealous Money got when he would talk to other females around her, and so did Juwan.

"You gon' have Money kill one of them bitches you fuckin' wit'. She's really feelin' you, bro. I knew that when we first met," Juwan said, passing Taelor a blunt filled with 'Dro. They were sitting at a table in a trap house, compressing and weighing work.

"Bro, she like my sister. Y'all's moms calls me her son," Taelor replied, inhaling 'Dro smoke into his lungs. He pounded his fist to his chest. The exotic marijuana had made him cough, forcing him to exhale.

"Yea, like a son-in-law, homie. Plus, Money ain't tryna hear that brotha shit! You should take her to a movie or some shit," Juwan suggested. Taelor knew her was going to really talk to Money about their relationship, so he immediately left Juwan to go find Money.

It didn't take him long to find her. He was nervous when he saw her walking on the block, but he knew he had to change Money's mind about getting to him. So, he sat in the car for a few minutes to get his thoughts together, before he approached her.

"What's up, Money?"

"I can't call it, what's up with you? Money retorted before pulling Taelor in for a hung.

"Not shit. Thought we could hang out."

"Hang out and do what?"

"Maybe we can do dinner and a movie."

“Dinner and a movie? Is this supposed to be a date or something?” Money inquired, trying not to show too much excitement.

“Naw. We just two friends hanging out.” Although Taelor could see that his response hurt Money a little, he knew he had to keep things a buck with her.

“Aight. I guess we can go,” Money spoke with sadness in her voice. She tried her best to wear a smile so Taelor wouldn’t catch that this statement had bothered her.

They rode in silence the first few minutes of their trip before Taelor decided to break the silence. "You know this will never work, don't you?" Taelor chattered. The comment wiped the smile right off Money's face.

"We can make it work. You just don't want it to work," Money said.

"Who told you I wanted a girlfriend in the first place? I don't need no girl.”

"You right, you don't need no girlfriend; you need a woman," Money responded, tossing her head to one side.

"Oh, you the woman I need? You haven't even graduated yet."

"We graduate this year."

"We? I'm not goin' back to school," Taelor muttered. "See, I told you that you need a woman. YOU ARE GOING BACK TO SCHOOL! I'ma help you get'cha diploma, Tae."

Taelor got quiet, and studied the firm expression on Money's face. "See, Money, that's what I'm talkin' 'bout. See, you's a straight-A student. You're good at school. Me, I'ma street nigga..."

"You sound stupid, but I know ya not stupid." Money stopped Tae from downgrading himself.

"I'm just sayin', Money, you don't need no boyfriend like me. I ain't no good fo' you. Niggas like me go to jail fo' a long time, or end up dead. I've accepted them terms, can you?"

"Mm-hm, I can accept them, but I will not allow either of us to be satisfied with that."

"Look! Money... you deserve mo'."

"I want you. Look, Tae, what I'm saying is, I know those outcomes are inevitable, but you don't have to settle for those two outcomes. As a street person, as you call yourself, you actually have a better chance of making something more of yourself. Us 'regular' folks have to depend on loans and worry about interest rates. You, on the other hand, are out here making thousands and thousands of dollars every day. That's not common for a seventeen-year-old. You can take some of that money and invest it. You can use the game as a stepping stone instead of a grave stone."

Tae listened in deep contemplation. Money had his attention, and was making a lot of sense.

"Instead of making thousands, you could be making millions the right way. You don't have to die from doing this, or go to jail if you plan right. And the only way to plan right is to go back to school," Money continued, saying all of the right things.

"See, I don't like nobody tryna change me. Plus, you on some jealous shit. I'm out here livin'. I ain't tryna be tied down." Tae's mind scrambled for more excuses.

"Whatever, Tae! I don't care about ya lil bitches. And I ain't tryna tie you down. I just want the best for you."

"And you the best fo' me?" Tae asked.

"Yes, I am the best for you. Tae, you can do whatever you want. I don't care about whatever girls you're messing with. Just be there for me when I need you. Just put me before all your other bitches. When I call, when I want you... come! I don't care what your ass is into, or who you're with."

After their date, Tae made up in his mind that he was going back to school. Especially, since all he had left were a few months. Money vowed to help him maintain passing grades and Tae let her know off the bat that he was going to continue to see other women. Money was hip to the shit and decided that "two could play that game" and decided that she was get her a man on the side.

****

It had been a month and Money had started seeing another baller named Mar Mar.

Mar Mar was from Garfield, which was on the East side of Pittsburgh. He owned a salon and a rib shack, and drove a Bentley Spur. Seeing this made Tae jealous. Money had stopped answering his calls, and was spending more time with Mar Mar.

"Yo, what's up wit' you an' that nigga you been hangin' out wit'?" Tae asked Money while they walked in the hallways of their school.

"What you mean?"

"You know what I mean, Money."

"Look at you. Now, you worried about who I'm seeing. You ain't care before when you was running around with all these other bitches and fucking all these dirty hoes."

"See, here you go. I thought you ain't care."

"No, here you go." Money got quiet for a minute. "You know I care."

"If you really fuck wit' me like that, you'd help me jack that nigga. I saw him picking you up in a Bentley. He got a lot of money." Tae asked, "You fuckin' that nigga?"

"NO! I'm not fuckin' nobody. Did I fuck you?"

"Nah. I was just checkin' to see if you was still a virgin. I thought he might have popped that cherry."

"Bye, Tae!"

"Nah! No, look. I'm sorry," Tae said, reaching out to grab her. "I'm sorry!"

"Hmph!" Money crossed her arms across her chest, and pouted. She was saving herself for him, and didn't appreciate his disrespectful comments.

"Look, this is what I'll do. If you help me get that nigga, I'll cut all my bitches off and just be wit' you."

"Are you going to finish school?"

"Yea, if you keep helping me," Tae said, looking down at the hallway floor.

"A'ight, let me find out where he keeps all his money at. He don't really trust me right now. Look, tho', Tae, I'ma help you, but you better not kill him. I'm not trying to live with that on my conscience," Money told Tae.

Once Tae agreed that he would finish school, Money has agreed that she would help him. By the time they stepped outside the school, they noticed that Mar Mar had pulled up and had stood outside his car waiting for Money to come out.

"Hey baby," Money greeted Mar Mar.

"Hey boo, you ready to go to the mall like I promised you last night?"

"Yes baby. Let's ride," Money commented just as Mar Mar opened the door for her, then jogged around to his side of the car and getting in. He crunk the car up and they headed to Monroeville mall listening to the latest Gucci Mane cd.

The went to damn near every store in the mall getting any and everything that they wanted. Money started to get hungry and asked if they could grab something from the food court. Of course, Mar Mar obliged her as he always did.

As they sat there eating, Mar Mar opened his mouth to speak, breaking the silence. "All this shoppin' and shit, when you gon' let a nigga hit some'in'? I've been waitin' fo' over a min now. You know I gotta like you 'cause I don't play this 'No sex game'," Mar Mar boldly stated.

"It ain't like you don't get nothing. I suck ya dick," Money said, rolling her eyes and neck.

"Yea, but I'm tryna get some of that pussy. Why you holdin' out?"

"When you learn to trust me, I'll give you some."

"Trust you? I do trust you."

"We've been dating for a while now, and we still going to hotels just to hang out. You must have a wife at home or something."

"A wife, tho'? Hell no, you trippin'. I'm tryna make you my wife."

"Yea, okay. If you was tryna make me your wife, I would be going to your house, and not a hotel every time we hook up."

"You wanna go to my spot? Come on, I'll take you," Mar Mar said, getting up from the table.

Fifteen minutes later, Mar Mar's Bentley pulled up at a newly renovated mini-mansion that sat on two acres. "Wow, bae, this is your house?" Money asked. Her eyes lit up like a Christmas tree at the sight of the mansion.

"Yup. I was tryna wait until it was fully renovated

before I brought you here, but since ya in such a rush... There's a few things my contractors have to do, but this is it. Come on. Let me take you inside."

"Who's that?" Money asked. As soon as they got in the door, Money could hear a group of people talking somewhere in the near distance.

"That's my brother, sister-in-law, and their kids. They come over every weekend just to kick it. I don't mind 'cause don't nobody else ever be here. I'm a loner, you know?"

"A loner, huh? What about me?"

"You're right. I guess I ain't no loner no mo'. But, I got four bedrooms, two bathrooms, two half bathrooms, a custom-built media center in the family room and all top of the line appliances, so I hope you can cook."

"Yes, I can cook."

"Good. So, you can cook fo' me and our kids."

"Un-un, hold up now. I'm just getting in the door."

"You right. But, um, I got a rear hot tub and dipping pool. You know, a lil some'in' some'in'. So, you ready to step things up? This is just part of what I have to offer," Mar Mar said as he paused, and took Money into his arms. "So, you ready to be my wifey?" he asked.

Money nodded her head... Yes.

"That's what's up." Mar Mar kissed Money. "So, you ready to see our bedroom?" Mar Mar asked with a smile on his face.

"Yea. You can show it to me, but I ain't doin' nothin' right now," Money asserted.

"Come on. Why you still playin'?"

"Be patient. I got you. Just not right now."

CHAPTER 2:

TENDER LOVING

It had been a week since Money had promised herself to Mar Mar. She liked him, but Taelor was who she really wanted. Money and Tae were set up to watch a movie at Tae's Bellevue spot. Suddenly, Money grabbed Tae's hand, and led him into the bedroom. The light from beyond the door created a silhouette of their images holding each other. Money was ready to give herself to Tae. She knew that if she continued to hold out on Mar Mar, he would either take her virginity, or she would be forced to lose to please Tae. With her agreeing to set Mar Mar up, Tae had kept his word, and had given up all his side pieces. At least, that's what Money believed, so now she wanted to share herself with the only man she had ever loved besides her brother.

"What?" Tae asked, face to face with Money.

Money walked over to the bed, and Tae finally realized what Money's eyes and body language were trying to tell him.

"Oh shit! You... you..."

Money nodded her head.... Yes.

“You sure? I don't want to pressure you."

"Ssshhh." Money put her finger to his mouth to hush Tae.

Tae moved in closer to Money, and pecked her on the lips, the forehead, and neck.

Money took Tae's face into both of her hands, and kissed him passionately for several seconds. She sashayed in a sexy manner over to the bedroom dresser, and lit two scented candles, then she pressed play on an iPod that was cradled on its port, and an old school slow jam mix started playing Jodeci's song *Forever My Lady.*

Forever, forever, forever

So, you're having my baby

And it means so much to me

There's nothing more precious

Than to raise a family

Money walked slowly back towards Tae, unraveling her paisley-print, silk chiffon top. She let it fall to the floor as Jodeci continued to set the mood.

If there's any doubt in your mind

You can count on me

Watching Money, Tae kicked off his Evisu sneakers, and loosened the belt holding up his Evisu jeans, never removing his eyes from Money's 34DD breasts which were contained by her Frederick's of Hollywood bralette.

I'll never let you down

Lady believe in me

Unzipping Tae's Bathing Ape's hoodie, Money took it off him and let it hit the floor, kissing him passionately again.

You and I

Will never fall apart

You and I

We knew right from the start, baby, baby

The day

We fell so far in love

Now our baby is born, healthy and strong

Now our dreams are reality

Forever my lady

Grabbing Money by her legs, Tae hoisted her up, and Money wrapped her legs around his waist.

"Please be gentle," Money told Tae.

Tae walked her to the bed and let her fall softly upon it. Sitting up at the edge of the bed with Tae standing in front of her, Money wedged his pants down and Tae's erection popped out at her.

"What a pleasant surprise," she said, looking at part of Tae's manhood that was partially exposed through the slit of his boxers. Digging his huge pussy-slayer out of its hole, she grabbed Tae by the backside, and filled her mouth up with it, taking in as much of it as she could. Her mouth was warm. She sucked on his dick, and licked around the crown of it as she looked at him with her cock-sucking eyes.

Tae had his head back, looking upward at the

ceiling. "Oooh, baby!"

Money's neck pecked back and forth, nice and slow. Tae looked down at Money as his monstrous pussy-slayer slid in and out of her dick eater. "Oh, no you don't. You ain't makin' me cum yet," Tae said, pulling his dick back from Money's dripping mouth. She scooted forward, wanting his dick back in her mouth. She never took her eyes off it.

Tae gently pushed Money back onto the bed, and pulled her printed boyfriend-fit jeans off, then her thong as she lifted her buttocks off the king-sized mattress, slowly revealing her shaven cunt. Its lips were fat, and her clit stuck out like a sore thumb.

"What are you doing?" Money asked as Tae turned her on her stomach.

"Shut up. Just put that ass in the air, and spread that ass," Tae instructed. Money did what she was told, and there she sat, face down on the bed with her ass tooted up.

Parting her ass cheeks, Tae licked up and down her dick-gobbling slit. He even tongued her asshole. "Tae," Money let out. "Mm, daddy!" Her face being buried into the pillow muffled her moans. Tae ate her ass, and fingered her tight pussy. "Oooh, aw," she groaned.

"You want me to stop?" Tae asked.

"Un-un," Money grunted as she shook her head no.

Tae continued to maneuver his finger in and out of her tight spot, trying to force his stiff tongue into her ass.

"Mmm... Oh... Tae... Tae," Money expressed the pleasure she felt.

Driving his tongue up the crack of her ass, Tae began to kiss Money's lower back, moaning as he did it. His throbbing dick dripped pre-cum, and Money's pussy was dripping wet. Kneeling behind her, Tae took a hold of his ten-and-a-half-inch shaft, and ran it up and down Money's drenched cum slit. It sent a tingling sensation up her spine, then Tae tried to enter her. The tip of his dick was round and wide as a half dollar. It made Money flinch.

"Oooh... Oooh." Money felt her pussy being spread. It hurt a little, but she didn't want Tae to stop.

"You want me to stop?" Tae asked again.

"NO!" Money cried out. "Keep goin'," she told Tae, but Tae stopped anyway.

"What? Why you stop?" Money looked back and asked Tae. With her ass still in the air, she was begging to be fucked good.

"Turn over," Tae told her, and again, Money did as she was told.

The piano of Force MD's *Tender Love* began to play.

Here I lay all alone

Tossin' turnin'

Longing for some of your

Tender love

Tae took Money's right foot into his hands, and

began to massage it, and Money threw her head back, completely relaxed. Then her head popped up, and her eyes opened wide. The feeling of Tae's soft, wet tongue slipping between each of her pedicured toes made her react this way.

I'm waitin' for the right

Moment to come

So I can thank you for

All the tender love you've given to me

Money's pussy juices oozed out of her cunt, the clear fluid leaking down between her ass cheeks. "Oh, that feels so good, Tae."

Then Tae applied a little pressure to the center of her foot, and made her toes spread apart. One by one, he sucked her toes, starting with the big toe.

Tender love (tender love)

Love so tender (ah)

"Mmmm... Oooh, Tae... Taaae, baby," Money moaned. Slowly, she ran her hand down her tight, six-pack abdominal, and started rubbing her clit in a circular motion with the middle finger of her right hand.

Tae stopped licking and sucking her toes to ask, "That feel good?"

"Ooo, yes, baby. Yes!" Money said, slipping her hot-pink colored finger tips in and out of her pleasure hole.

Holdin' me close to you

Baby I surrender

Tae stopped sucking Money's toes and kissed up her foot, and up her inner thigh until his mouth met the destination of her pulsating pussy.

Money fed Tae her pussy juice from her dripping fingers. He licked all over them, then he pulled back the hood of her clit, and used the tip of his tongue to drive her completely insane. Tae's tongue flickered back and forth on her clit.

"Oh, fuck, fuck... FUUUCCK!" Money had her first orgasm. Seeing her creamy white fluids oozing out of her pussy made Tae really go crazy. Snaking his head wildly, he took two fingers and plugged her tight hole with them. He moved them in and out of her and Money fucked them back, panting as she thrust her pelvis. Thinking of the joy she felt having her first orgasm made her fuck his fingers harder and faster. She was ready to be fucked, and Tae knew it, but took his time pleasing her. It was her first time, and he wanted to please her.

Money's body began to tremble, her eyes rolled to the back of her head, she bit her bottom lip, then she screamed out, "TAAAE!" She was having another orgasm. This time, her fluids squirted out of her pussy.

"What the fuck! Did you piss?" Tae pulled his head back and asked.

Money couldn't say a word. She could barely shake her head no. "No... No... I came," she finally let out.

"Damn, you squirted," Tae said, working his fingers back into her pussy. "I want you to do it again. Squirt in my mouth," he told Money, and she nodded her head.

Fingering her harder and faster while licking her clit made Money start to scoot backward. "Uh-uh, get back here!" Tae told her, putting her legs on his shoulders. He wrapped his arms around her thighs so she could no longer run from him, but he was eating her pussy so well that she couldn't help but fight him. She tried pushing his head away from her pussy, but Tae wanted her to squirt again.

"Put it in, Tae. Put it in," Money begged. She couldn't take any more of his head game; it was too good. "PUT IT IN, TAE. I'M READY, TAE." She grabbed his head.

"You ready fo' the dick? You sure?"

"Yes," Money said.

Kissing up her body, Tae could feel her body trembling. She purred like a fluffy, white kitten. He took each breast, one by one, and licked each nipple. "Oh... ooh." Every part of Money's body was sensitive.

Kissing up her neck, Tae took a hold of his dick, and ran it up and down Money's wet pussy. Even that drove her crazy, and her legs jerked.

Then Tae let his dick go. "You put it in," he told Money, looking her in the face. She felt exhausted. Her eyes were slanted, her body was covered in sweat, and her pussy was creamy.

Taking a hold of Tae's ten and a half inch, throbbing

cock, she guided it into her wetness. Cautiously, Tae pushed inside of her. "Ooh, don't stop. Put it all in me. Do it slow. Do it slow, Tae." Her pussy was a very tight fit for Tae's large, Python-like prick. "Mmmm," Money groaned. "I want you to fuck this pussy real good, okay, Tae?"

"Mm-hm," Tae replied, easing his dick into her inch by inch, only stopping when he felt Money's fingertips claw into his back. "Ahh!" Tae shrieked.

"Sorry, baby."

"Just get on top of me, and put it in," Tae said, getting on his back.

Money climbed on top of him, and eased Tae's dick into her a few inches at a time.

Tae took a hold of her hips, and forced a few more inches of himself into her. "Go down on it," he told her as he popped his hips, driving his dick into her as if he was trying to knock down a wall. Money's body jerked as he did so, then Tae grabbed her, and flipped her back onto her back with his dick still in her.

"Oooh," Money moaned.

"Ssshh." Now it was Tae's turn to hush her.

"Mm-mm-mm." Money grabbed Tae by his waist. She wanted all of him inside of her. "Do it harder," Money told Tae.

Tae began to go to work on the pussy. He had his arms braced on the outside of her, lifting himself off her just enough for them to watch his dick going in and out. "MMM-HMM, yesss. Harder! Harder!"

Tae pounded.

"Harder! Harrrd-errr! Tear this pussy up. Tear this pussy up!"

"I'ma tear this pussy up!" Tae was in a zone.

"YES. YES, DADDY. Tear it up. Cum in me... Cum in me!"

"You wanna baby? Huh? Huh?"

"Yes, yes... put a baby in meee. Put a baby in meee."

"Turn over, I want it from the back," Tae said, flipping Money over, then he guided his dick into her hot spot like a heat-seeking missile. His plans were to be gentle at first, but Money wanted him to punish her.

Reaching his arm around to the front of Money, Tae fingered her cunt while he fucked her from behind. "Yesss!" Money moaned loudly.

Tae's hips thrust with more and more momentum. Money turned her head, and she and Tae kissed. The position was awkward, but felt so good to both of them. "Faster... Harder!" Money demanded, making Tae force more and more of himself into her. As more and more of his thick slab of meat jammed into her pretty, tight hole, Money gasped for breath, and Tae felt an extra wetness seep out of her pussy. The harder he fucked her, the more he felt the wetness cover his abdomen. He knew that he had popped her cherry, but he was too into fucking her to stop.

"Oooh... Tae... My God!" Money cried out.

"Damn, that pussy's so wet," Tae said, grabbing Money by the hips, and driving her face into the pillow. With each thrust, he punished and violated her virginity. Gripping Money's 34-24-41 frame, he worked a rhythm that made him feel like he was about to cum.

Money tossed her head back and forth, and she moaned and begged him not to stop. Eventually, tears of pleasure streamed down her face. She loved Tae that much.

SMACK! "This what you want?" *SMACK!* "This what you want?" Tae asked, smacking Money's ass as he fucked her doggy-style.

"Yes. Yes, baby. Smack that ass! Smack it!"

SMACK! Tae smacked her ass again as Money started throwing her ass back. "Yes, yes, Tae. Yesss!" Money bleated, tossing her ass backward with more force. Tae drove his lengthy rod into her until his balls slapped and bounced off the thickness of her mischievous beaver.

Tae slowly pulled his dick out of her, and slammed back into her. Gradually pulling out, he rammed his rod into her again before pulling out again, leaving just the tip inserted. He pounded into her three times repeatedly.

"OH, OH, OH!" Money felt every inch of him inside of her. Clenching the bed sheets with both hands, she tried to brace herself, but Tae pounded her pussy until she lay flat on the bed, but that didn't stop him.

"You want this pussy beat up, huh?"

"Mm, yes! Mm, yes! Tae... Taaae... Taaaaae," she

cried her lover's name as she experienced her third orgasm. "I'm cummin'. I'm cummin'. Shiiit! I-I-I'm cuuuummmin'!" Money roared.

Tae's pumps became calculated. "You cummin', baby?" Money asked, feeling Tae's hot cum shoot up inside of her.

"Mmm-hm," Tae responded as his ass cheeks clenched. Both of their bodies quivered and Tae's arms buckled. They couldn't withstand his body weight. He collapsed on top of Money, and then he rolled off her. "Damn, bae," he said, looking over at Money. They both panted, neither could utter a syllable at the moment.

Tae reached for Money. "Babe?"

"No, don't... t-touch me." Money was too sensitive to touch. She just wanted to lay there for a minute or at least until the quivering was over.

Tae backed away from her, and reached down, feeling the thick wetness drying on his abdomen and crotch. "Bae, I think ya spottin'," Tae said.

"What you mean?" Money turned over and asked. Tae's statement had thrown her off.

"I think ya spottin'," Tae repeated, but he was sure that she was.

"WHAT?" Money got up, and ran to the light switch and turned it on. "Eeeewww!" She turned the light back off. "I'm so fuckin' embarrassed!" Money said, running to the bathroom.

CHAPTER 3:

JACK BOY COME UP

Mar Mar had finally slipped up, and Money had overheard him talking business on the phone. Beforehand, she had spent close to forty minutes sucking his dick and swallowing his cum. Afterwards, they fell asleep, and around 3:00 A.M., they were both awakened by his cell phone ringing, but Money pretended to still be asleep.

Mar Mar stepped into the hallway to take the call. "You need me to meet you, or are you comin' to the crib? Cool, you gon' bring it here? A'ight, tomorrow night at ten," Money had overheard him saying.

This could be big. I gotta tell Tae, Money thought to herself, still laying in the bed, faking a light snore.

Mar Mar got back into the bed and wrapped his arms around her. "Mm, you okay, baby?" Money asked.

"Yea. That was my man. I got something to do tomorrow night. I might need ya help," Mar Mar told Money. Normally, he used his brother's wife to take his work to his stash spot, but now that Money had earned his trust, he wanted to start using her.

He had purposely left large sums of money laying around her, and she had never asked for a dollar or taken any of it. To him, that proved that she was not a money-hungry bitch, and Mar Mar liked that.

"Tomorrow's goin' to be a special night. You should make it better by giving me some of that pussy," Mar Mar said.

"I was thinking the same thing. I think I'm ready fo' that dick. You've been good to me," Money lied to him.

"Worrrddd! Come on, we should get it poppin' now."

"No, bae. Not now. I'm tired from suckin' ya dick. I got you after you handle ya business. It'll be like a celebration. I promise."

"YOU PROMISE?" Mar Mar repeated with a smile on his face. He was happy that he was finally going to have sex with Money. Her head game was bomb, but he wanted to fuck her. Maybe even get her pregnant.

"Yes, baby. I promise. Now, let's go back to sleep," Money said, clasping his arms under hers.

"That's what I'm talkin' 'bout. Hey, tomorrow, I'ma need you to drive something somewhere," Mar Mar whispered to Money.

"Okay, babe. Whatever you want, I got you," Money said in a groggy voice.

"That's my baby," Mar Mar said, kissing the back of Money's head. He loved how down she was.

****

The day of the jack had finally arrived. Tae knew that he would need help. Money being caught up in the middle of the jack, meant that he couldn't ask her brother for help. Juwan would never approve of his sister being used as bait, so Tae called his friend, Jesse "JB" Beasley. He was another O.G. from the Northside.

The day after Mar Mar had taken Money to his estate, Money told Tae where he lived, and how it was laid out inside and out. So, he was familiar with the township. The thing that concerned Tae was how the cops patrolled the area periodically.

Nine P.M. THAT NIGHT, Tae and JB put one in the air on the way to do the jack. Project Pat's *Layin' Da Smack Down* CD played as they drove there.

"Look, nigga, no matter what happens, don't kill nobody. We only goin' to get that paper, and Money's up there, so be careful," Tae told JB.

"Money's up there?"

"Yea, this is her move."

“What? Get the fuck outta here. Not school girl."

"Hell yea."

"Oh, that's why Frosty ain't here wit' us," JB said, calling Juwan by his new street name, which he had gotten because he was flooding the streets with blow, and was always draped in over a hundred thousand dollars’ worth of iced-out jewelry.

"Frosty can't know about this. You feel me?" Tae told JB.

"I got you. So, how we gon' do this?"

"Look, dude gotta nice lil wooded area around his spot. We gon' park, and make our way through the woods to his spot and lay in the woods until we see some'in'. Soon as the connect pulls up wit' the work, we jump out on their asses," Tae said, taking the blunt from JB and hitting it. "Money got her ears open, so soon as she hears some'in', she gon' text us. Shit should go smooth," Tae continued, blowing smoke into the air.

"How many niggas we talkin' 'bout?" JB asked.

"I ain't sure. That's why we gotta hit 'em wit' the element of surprise and lay they asses down quickly! But if it's too many niggas, we just gon' fall back fo' a minute."

At 10:30 p.m., they were parked up outside, staking out Mar Mar's house.

"What the fuck, bruh? It's like 10:30," JB whispered as they watched Mar Mar's driveway through the darkness of the woods that surrounded his luxurious estate.

"Hol' up, this Money right here," Tae said, pressing the answer button. "Yo, we right outside." He listened briefly before hanging up.

"Dude 'bout to pull up now," he told JB, cocking his strap back.

JB cocked the slide back on his weapon also, then they pulled their masks over their faces and waited.

"We should try to get under that nigga's whip," JB said, observing Mar Mar's Bentley in the driveway.

"Naw. It's too late. That's too risky. That nigga might have cameras. He might be watchin' the outside of his shit," Tae told him.

It wasn't even two minutes later, that a Kia Sedona pulled into Mar Mar's driveway.

"Let's get it," JB said, ready to move out, but Tae stopped him.

"No, JB, wait fo' dude to come out to meet his plug before we move out."

A few seconds later, Mar Mar did just that. "Hey, bruh, you gettin' out?" Mar Mar asked the plug when the two masked men brandishing their gats ran up.

"PUT YA HANDS UP! PUT YA HANDS UP, MUTHAFUCKAS!!"

"What the—"

POP! "Nigga, stop runnin' fo' I fill ya ass up wit' this lead!" JB yelled as he let of a warning shot, stopping Mar Mar in his tracks. Seeing the two of them emerge from the woods had spooked him, and he tried to run back into the house.

"Nigga, don't even try me! See that dot on ya head? Don't make me put a bullet to it!" Mar Mar's plug tried to reach for his strap, but Tae stopped him.

"Yo! Get that nigga's strap, and get that bitch-ass nigga's strap, too. I know he got one," Tae said, talking about Mar Mar.

"Give it up," JB said, disarming Mar Mar. A'ight, yours, too, you bitch-ass nigga!" JB demanded to the plug.

"Now march y'all asses in the house. It's time to play find the dope and money, muthafuckas," Tae told Mar

Mar and his connect, but to their surprise, Money stood at the entrance in her bra, panties and silk robe, holding a AK-47. "Drop y'all muthafuckin' guns!" Money yelled out, shaking as she aimed the assault rifle at JB and Tae.

"Bitch, is you crazy? I'll blow ya nigga's brains all over ya pretty lil face," JB said.

"Now put'cha choppa down!" Tae hollered.

"Yo! You betta put that muthafuckin' choppa down, bitch!" JB gave Money his final warning. He didn't know what was going on. Seeing Money pointing an AK at them confused him, and made him nervous.

"Babe, just put it down. I'ma just give these niggas what they came fo'," Mar Mar said, shrugging his shoulders, and shaking his head.

"See, now that's what I'm talkin' 'bout," Tae said.

"Now give me the choppa," JB said, slowly walking over to Money with piercing eyes.

"Just give it to him," Mar Mar told Money.

"You betta listen to ya man," JB said as he took the choppa off of Money, then he struck her with it and motioned like he was going to hit her again.

"Oof!" was the sound Money made as she toppled backward.

"No, man. NO! Stop! I'll give you everything, just don't kill us!"

After Mar Mar's safe had been cleaned out, the

plug, Mar Mar and Money laid on the bedroom floor with their hands zip-tied behind their backs. Tae made sure Money's zip-tie was loose enough for her to free herself. "Ugh, I-I think I can get loose," Money said after the masked jackers left. She wiggled her hand out of the black, plastic band wrapped around her wrists. Watching Money squirm herself loose, the plug tried to do the same, but was unable to. His zip-ties were too tight. All the while, though, he never took his eyes off the AK-47 the jackers had left behind.

"There, I'm out," Money said, finally free. She stood up and rubbed her wrists.

"Cut me loose, babe," Mar Mar told Money.

Money looked around the bedroom for something to cut the zip-ties with. Taking a pair of scissors, she cut the connect loose first because he was the closest to her, then she cut Mar Mar loose.

"Who was that?" the plug asked.

"I don't—hol' up... What the..." Mar Mar attempted to answer the connect's question, but was at a loss for words when he turned to see the plug pointing the AK-47 at him and Money. Money ran out of the room, and a volley of bullets followed her out of the bedroom, tearing holes through the bedroom walls.

Mar Mar was frozen in his tracks. The plug had the assault rifle pointed at him. "I think you set me the fuck up!" the plug said to Mar Mar with a menacing look on his face.

"Are you crazy? Why would I do some dumb shit

like that, and why would I jack myself?"

"You know I had more than just ya work in the van, and you're gettin' all ya shit back. Yea, you thought this fake-ass jack move would work, but I'm too smart for this shit!"

"Naaaw, dawg. Come on, now. You know me. You know I'm not gonna try no weak shit like that."

"One of you two did this shit," the plug said as he lifted the AK and aimed it at Mar Mar.

"Come on, bruh, you know—" Those were Mar Mar's last words as the plug let off a barrage of shots, hitting Mar Mar in his upper body, splitting his chest wide open, and tearing a chunk out of his skull.

Hearing the gunshots, Money ran into the woods with her cell phone in hand.

Looking around the bedroom, the plug searched for Mar Mar's car keys. Patting Mar Mar's pockets, he felt what he believed were them. "Got 'em." He knew that the gunshots had been heard, and the police were on their way, so he hurried. He wasn't thinking about Money getting away because once he got away, he knew they would see each other again.

Picking up the AK, he ran outside to Mar Mar's car. As he expected, his van was gone. JB and Tae had planned on getting to a place where they could strip it down to its stash spots and then burn it. In total, the plug had lost his cell phone, his number one worker, and twenty kilos of cocaine.

Out of breath, Money scurried through the woods as she called Tae.

"Money!" Tae answered.

"Come get me. I'm scared, Tae. He's tryna kill me," Money frantically told Tae. Gazing from the darkness of the wooded area, she could see the plug exit Mar Mar's mansion, and get into his Bentley, but as he was pulling off, the police were pulling up. The police spoke over the car's loudspeaker, "Turn the car off!"

"Where are you?" Tae asked Money, hearing the policeman's demand in the background.

"I'm in the woods. The police got the connect pulled over."

The plug fired into the police car, fatally wounding its driver.

POP! POP! POP! The police officer on the passenger side of the cruiser exited the car and fired three rounds into the plug, killing him instantly. Sheltered on the side of the cruiser, the officer radioed in, "Officer down!"

"Oooh, no, they killed him!" Money broke down, witnessing her first murders.

"MONEY? MONEY? Tae yelled into the phone. Money didn't say a word, but Tae could hear her sobbing. "I'm on my way to get you."

"They killed him," Money said in disbelief.

"The cops killed who, Money?"

"The connect. They killed the connect."

"I'm on my way back. Go through the woods until you see the street. Don't come out of the woods 'til you see me. I'll be there in a few minutes," Tae said.

He hung up with Money and called JB. "The cops killed the plug. I'm turnin' around to get Money. Take the van to the spot. I'll be right behind you."

"Got you. Say no mo'," JB replied.

****

Three years had passed since the hit. Smack Down exited the shower at his Edgewood Estate, where he went almost every night. It was one of the places he went to escape the street life. Staring at himself in the steamy bathroom mirror, he ran his fingers over the two bullet wounds in his chest, thinking about the gunfire that had nearly taken his life. The near-death experience came courtesy of Mr. Frosty Blow's strap.

After stumbling upon his sister's large stash of money, Mr. Frosty Blow forced a confession out of Money, which explained Tae's newfound success, and his sister being questioned by homicide detectives. He was told that her boyfriend had died during a home invasion, but he didn't know that Tae was behind it, and had used his sister to set it all up.

After Money and Tae's graduation, Money stayed confined to her bedroom, paranoid and pregnant. She didn't want to be bothered by anyone, not even Tae. Mr. Frosty Blow thought it was because she had lost her boyfriend, but he had finally gotten the truth out of her, and now knew why she was acting so strange.

Hearing every detail about the jack, except JB's name, Mr. Frosty Blow replayed everything that had taken place after her boyfriend's death in his head.

Tae had claimed he had found a new connect, and had served him several kilos for a cheaper price than he was getting them for. He had bought matching Bentleys for he and Money, moved into a baby mansion, and had bought a state-of-the-art studio. He had even changed his name to "Smack Down," and started rapping, inspired by his favorite rapper, Project Pat.

Mr. Frosty Blow rushed to Smack Down's studio after he had heard everything, and everything set in. Seeing Smack Down in the studio, Mr. Frosty Blow pulled his strap and shot Smack Down twice, leaving him slumped in the corner of the recording booth.

"Fuckin' studio gangsta," was all Tae recalled Mr. Frosty Blow saying after waking up from his operation. He was surrounded by family and friends, including a teary-eyed Money. What Money had left out of the story she had told her brother was that she was pregnant, and five months later, their son was born.

Shortly after the birth of her son, Money and a friend of hers exited the Century Three Mall. As they approached Money's Bentley, a man came out of nowhere and opened fire on Money. "This is for Mar Mar," said the shooter before fleeing.

Thinking about him and Money's past, Smack Down stared at the image of himself in the foggy mirror and shook his head. He thought about how far they had come, and if no one understood, he understood that every action caused a reaction. Smack Down shook his head and turned from the mirror.

"Dad?" Smack Down's son, Octavius, called out. "Ma wants you," the thirteen-year-old told his father.

Tae went into the bedroom, and glanced at Money as she sat up in the bed. She looked prettier than ever. "You ready?" Tae asked. It was Money's big day. She was pitching the idea of a reality show to one of the biggest moguls in the city of Pittsburgh.

"Yes, I'm ready to sign my first multi-million-dollar deal. Are you ready to be a reality TV star?" Money asked Smack Down with a huge smile on her face.

"No, not really, but I'll do anything fo' you, you know that, bae."

Placing his arms around Money's body, he hoisted her up. Money wrapped her arms around his neck, and braced herself as he sat her in her automatic wheelchair.

Money's shooter had left her paralyzed. She had survived the shooting, but had lost the use of her legs.

Mr. Frosty Blow and Smack Down had joined forces to murder the man who had shot her, but they remained foes afterward. The only thing that kept either of them from killing one another was Octavius, and the love that Money shared between the two of them.

CHAPTER 4:

DEAL WORTH MULTI-MILLZ

At Monte Bucks Enterprises, entertainment mogul, Monte Bucks, stood inside of a boardroom where he conducted most of his business meetings. Several feet away from the plush chairs and boardroom table, he stared out of the glass at the sprouting water fountain inside of Pittsburgh's Point State Park, puffing on a Davidoff Blend with two massive Presa Canarios on each side of him, awaiting his every command.

His assistants stood around with clipboards, and his camera crew held giant lights, ready to shoot the meeting between him and his new business partner, Money King. She had pitched a Pittsburgh Hip Hop reality show called *Love & Trap Muzik, Pittsburgh*, and he agreed to invest five million into developing the show.

Normally, the billionaire would have been encircled by a fashionable, international crowd made up of top-name producers, muses, artists, media moguls, and models who gathered around for two thousand dollar shots of Louis XIII in the courtyard of the palace he called Bucks Plaza Hotel, but not today. On this particular day, it was all about Money King and their new baby, *Love & Trap Muzik, Pittsburgh.*

As a key figure, and part of an international elite group of industrialist, heiress, and playboys, he ping-ponged across the Atlantic, surfing global skies in luxurious Gulf Stream Jets.

Born in 1962 to a runaway teenage mother who

gave him away to his aunt and uncle, Monte Bucks pursued a singing career at an early age, pitching his demo to whomever would listen to it.

In the early eighties, he cashed his first million-dollar check, and led one of music's most influential groups, topping the charts with worldwide hits like, "Let Me Lace My Joint, With You" and a groovy dance number called "If He Can Have You, I Can Too." But, after its third tour, creative differences between the band members broke the Pittsburgh based group apart.

Not one to be stifled, Monte Bucks took his last two thousand dollars and co-founded Chalice Recordings with the group's keyboardist, Jimmy “Funky Fingers” Count, and they went on to write and produce smash hits that turned their record label into a multi-million-dollar company. After signing a hundred-million-dollar distribution deal with Sony, he expanded with an ancillary brand like Mega-Bucks gaming.

In 1997, with two platinum albums, and a dozen Grammys, he made a decision to leave the music industry. He sold his half of the company for $400 million, and invested in film and television production.

In 1998, using his entrepreneurial mentality, he partnered with Lionsgate and helped start Animax, an animation company that linked some of the world's highest paid artist to do the voice overs of some of the movie industry's most famous animated characters.

Using film and television as a platform, he purchased his own 200,000 square foot studio, and wrote, produced and directed his very first Blockbuster movie.

According to Forbes, in 2014, the Fortune 500 CEO's estimated worth was somewhere around 1.8 billion dollars, and now with thirty years of movie and music knowledge, the Pittsburgh native and visionary would almost single-handedly place his city on the reality TV map. Of course, with Money King's help. Together, they would give Pittsburgh's new generation of artist a chance to spotlight their talents on their reality television show.

Emanating a pervasive aroma of Chrome Intense, blended with the smell of sweet black licorice from his torpedo cigar, he inhaled and slowly exhaled its smoke from his curled lips into the atmosphere as he awaited Money King's arrival. His assistant had made him aware of her ascension from the elevator.

Moments later, Money King's electric wheelchair entered the boardroom. When she entered, the singer-mogul shook her hand, and invited her to the table where he had made most of his multi-million-dollar deals. Saturating his palate with the smoke of the Davidoff, he reclined in a chair that resembled a throne, fit for a king, ready to look over the list of artists who would be on the show, provided by and recommended by Money King.

This would be the first scene of *Love & Trap Muzik, Pittsburgh*, and the second meeting between the trap queen and lord of various business ventures. "There's our future," Money said as she watched her slender, athletic built, baldheaded, angular faced partner study the folder of artist she had provided.

"I had my staff bring you a Smartwater. If you want something stronger than that, let me know," Mr. Bucks said, gazing at Money with striking eyes through a cloud of scented smoke.

"No, thanks. This is fine," Money lied. She was nervous as hell. She wouldn't have minded a two-thousand dollar shot of Louis, and one of those beyond handsome male supermodels or media moguls he so often paraded around the world with. Instead, they were in the company of bobble headed assistants, cameramen, and two man-eaters named after the legendary rap group, The Dot & The Dub.

Pushing an ashtray and a v-cutter to the side, Mr. Bucks opened the folder that was in a leather embroidered case. "So, let's get on with it," he said, leaning back as he stroked his close shaven, salt-and-pepper goatee with one hand and his expensive torpedo in the other as he looked over the documentation.

SEXY DUVALL A.K.A. the sexiest entertainer on the planet: Local stripper with global clientele. Once a major player on BGC, she has fought the odds all her life and clawed her way to the top, all the while staying super sexy. Currently working at Club Reflection, Sexy Duvall has used her street savviness, and her 36-26-44, 5'2 frame to become a self-made millionaire.

MR. FROSTY BLOW: The hustler turned Trap Muzik god, claims to own the streets of Pittsburgh. With two platinum albums to date, he battles with rap rivals like Smack Down and street thugs alike to keep his crown, dodging the Feds, and their federal indictments.

SMACK DOWN: With just a month left before his fifth independent album release, the Smack Dizzy Boyz's boss has blessed his fans with a hundred freestyles videos in one week, racking up twenty million views on YouTube. As a battle rapper, he goes at some of the top artist in the industry and steps on and destroys underground rappers in the streets. With braggadocio sixteens, he crushes and kills all competition on the way to the top. In doing so, Smack Down has attracted record labels and executives to himself like vultures to a dead carcass. Caught up in a multi-million-dollar bidding war, the gritty, underground king has to decide between staying in the streets and the industry.

DOMINICAN FLAMES: Hailing all the way from Brooklyn, New York, Dominican Flames' parents made their way to Pittsburgh in the late eighties, where they faced federal indictments for drug distribution and racketeering, which they both received lengthy sentences for.

But now, the daughter of the Drug Lord Dynasty owns one of the biggest strip clubs in Pennsylvania, and manages strippers and upcoming rap artist like Sexy Duvall and her daughter, America.

DQ DAWG: A trap veteran turned author who has made millions in the music industry, and is currently taking over the publishing world one book at a time. Reinventing himself after a seven-year hiatus, the rapper once known as IL Zigga, has once again shot to the top of the charts with his new single, "She Like It From The Baaack!" Torn between his record contract and publishing deal, he manages to stay on top of both with a number one single and a number one urban novel, balancing both careers like a checkbook filled with zeroes.

BLOCKS N BRICKS: "Mr. Lived Through It All" is

taking on all comers, new and old. The son of one of Hip Hop's most revered lyricist, Dre Dog Ski, Blocks N Bricks carries the torch, scorching anybody who gets in his way as he blazes his way to Trap Muzik infamy in pursuit of the longevity and accolades that made his father a commercial and mainstream success.

MAKING HITZ: A high-caliber producer with ties to the music industry's most majestic couple, King and Queen Carter. At the head of his own record label, he helps artists get recognized and released, solidifying their penmanship on the lines of huge record deals.

The rapper, songwriter and producer is a triple threat. Starting as a pupil of legendary, female producer, Boom Bap's musical elite, the prodigy, Making Hitz, took Boom Bap's production advice and ran with it. With close to 200 chart-topping smashes to date in three short years, he has arrived and plans to conquer.

BOOM BAP: The Pittsburgh native is a legendary female producer who spends most of her time crafting timeless hits. In between producing and business meetings, the melodic mastermind behind the scene of some of the most adored records, sets aside the time to mentor rap idols and crooners alike, all the while continuing to captivate the ears of urban and pop audiences, decade after decade.

"Money, baby, it looks like we gotta winning line-up. I want to start recording the show right away, like, today. I wanna get this season out the way, and start season two and three A.S.A.P! I want heavy promo, online and in the streets. When we go to BET, I want them to cut us a big check," Mr. Bucks said.

"Say no more, I'm on it," Money said, using her cell phone to inform the cast that they would be recording for the show right away.

CHAPTER 5:

BANKROLL FRESH

All we do is trap, a1l we do is trap

A1l we do is trap, all we do is trap

I wouldn't be where I was at if I didn't fuckin' trap

I don't leave the trap, I stay down just to make it happen

Stay down to get it, grinded from a fifty

Then I got it up, I had my niggas wit' me.

Listening to Bankroll Fresh's *Trap*, Smack Down took a hammer to a kilogram of cocaine, then took a razor and cut into the duct tape the kilo was wrapped in. Removing several large blocks of cocaine from the kilo, he placed them on a scale, and weighed them until the scale read 126 grams. After placing the 4-1-2 into two thick Ziploc bags, he placed it on newspaper.

Smack Down pounded the work with the hammer some more, and used the bottom of his brown, transparent Visionware pot to crush the boulders into fine powder.

After Smack Down grinded the chunks of consolidated cocaine into powder, he prepped it to be cooked. Leaving the hammer, cocaine and pot on the floor, he ripped open a yellow box of baking soda, and poured what he believed to be four and a half ounces into a Ziploc bag. It was six grams short, so he added baking soda until the scale read 133 grams. He added an extra seven grams because he knew that at least seven grams would burn off in the cook.

Placing the Visionware pot on the stove, he ignited the fire under the pot, and put it on medium. Waiting for the powder to heat up, he stirred it, and crushed the remaining chunks of compressed cocaine that needed epitomized, then he added the baking soda, and stirred the powders together. He used a squirt gun and squirted a small amount of water on the product, the cocaine sizzled, and its aroma lit up the room. Once the work started to bubble, he used a butter knife to stir it up, and the cooking acetone made the kitchen smell of burning glue.

Working his wrist in a 360 motion, he watched as the oil and baking soda turned into a thick white paste. After turning off the fire, he plugged up the kitchen sink, took a bag of ice out of the freezer, dumped it into the sink, and ran a stream of cold water into the sink. Then, he placed the pot of cocaine into the sink, and watched it harden as he periodically rubbed pieces of ice on the bottom of the pot.

Using his hand, Smack Down scooped ice water into the pot. Once he was sure that the cocaine was hard, he used a toothbrush and scrubbed the baking soda residue off the cocaine, rinsed it, and turned off the water.

Taking a knife, he carefully stabbed into the pot of street product, and caused it to crack in several directions. Then he used the knife and maneuvered it around the border of the pot, separating the cocaine in large, chunky parts. Placing the large, chunky parts into a Ziploc bag, he weighed it, and watched as the numbers on the scale shot up to 254 grams. He had turned four and a half ounces into a quarter of a kilogram.

Ring! Ring! Ring!

“Yo, baby, how did the meeting go? Oh, okay, that’s what’s up. Yea, okay, I’m looking forward to it. Cool, let’s give the people a show. I'm proud of you, wifey," he said before ending the call.

Money had called Smack Down to put him on notice that he would be one of the first artists to film for the new reality show, *Love & Trap Muzik, Pittsburgh*.

Leaning back on the kitchen counter, he looked over at the cocaine he had just cooked up, and told himself, "I gotta make this reality TV shit work!"

In the living room, the Smack Dizzy Boyz were listening to Future, smoking Sour and popping pills. Smack Down demanded their attention. "Yo! Yo! Turn that shit down." After the music was turned down, he made his announcement. " Money just called and we start filming fo' that *Love & Trap Muzik* shit today or tomorrow. There's goin' to be a lot of competition on the show, so y'all know we gotta turn up at all times."

****

On the inside of Mr. Frosty Blow’s record label office, he held a boardroom meeting after he received a call from Money about the show.

"Two platinum albums and a nigga still haven't reached my goal. Three mill', four mill' ain't shit! You got rap niggas out here sittin' on two and three hunnid million.

Yea, shit look good from the outside—mansion, cars, bitches, the jewelry—but on the inside, it ain't right. That nigga B.I.G ain't die wit' a hunnid million, neither did that nigga Pac. Yea, them niggas is the best in the game, but I ain't tryna go out just the best in the game. I need to die comfortable, wit' at least a hunnid mill'. I need to be up when I go. A nigga got kids and shit. I'm talking generational paper. That's the type of paper I need y'all to help us get—help me get. Y'all wit' me?"

"YEEEAAAH!" the staff members howled.

"A'ight then! My sister just hit me and told me that we'll be recording fo' *Love & Trap Muzik, Pittsburgh*, so we gon' have to show all the other muthafuckas on the show and the world who run this city," Mr. Frosty Blow said as he paced back and forth as his onlookers took in his every word.

"This is the first season, so we gotta dominate! We gotta make boss moves. This might be the first and last show, so we gotta leave an impression on the world, you know? There's mad talent on the show. Niggas like DQ Dawg doin' his thang, Blocks N Bricks, that lame-ass nigga Smack Down and his boys, and a few other muthafuckas, but we gon' outdo 'em all," Mr. Frosty Blow said to encourage his team. He wanted to make sure they were all on point, and understood the importance of winning. "So, what we got lined up fo' the show?" he asked, taking a seat at the head of the boardroom table.

Armoni, his top assistant, looked through his notes and stood up. "We got you a listening session with the super-producer Boom Bap tomorrow night, and another one with Making Hitz. Both sessions can be recorded for the show."

"Okay. Sounds good," Mr. Frosty Blow said, nodding his head up and down. "What else?" he added, waiting to hear more.

"I know you're looking for a new sound, and at the same time, you want the promo, so I wanted you to be the first one on the show to meet with them. They're both hot right now," Armoni continued.

"That's what's up. And what about cars?"

"I got you a Lambo truck. I was goin' to get you the Bentley truck, but after I made several calls, I found out Blocks N Bricks will be drivin' that for the show, and I know you don't wanna be drivin' the same truck as him."

"Hell no! Good shit. Have you crosschecked our tour dates with the show's dates for filming?"

Armoni flipped through his notes. "I did, and we'll have to film around a few filming dates, or we can just film a few tour dates for the show. We gotta twenty-five-city tour coming up, and, one of your shows will be here in Pittsburgh.

"Dominican Flames called, and she wants you to perform at her club. She also wants it to be incorporated with *Love & Trap Muzik*. I guess she wants to use the footage as part of her intro on the show.

"That's it for now. I have to call ya sister and ask about promo as far as the show, and find out if we'll have to cover travel expenses while we're on tour an' shit."

"What about the stylist?"

"Oh yea, I forgot." Armoni thumbed through his notes. "Your stylist will be back from Cali tonight, so I'll set up a meeting."

"A'ight. Everything on point, and I want y'all to keep it that way. Make sure y'all keep y'all's ears to the streets. I wanna know what everybody on the show is doin'. Stay on top of 'em. I don't want none of these muthafuckas outdoin' us, especially that bitch-ass nigga Smack Down!"

CHAPTER 6:

REALITY TV STARS

A week into recording for Love and Trap Muzik, Pittsburgh, DQ Dawg and Sexy Duvall filmed at Reflection. While the cameras recorded, everyone inside acted as if they didn't exist.

DQ Dawg and Sexy Duvall were cued to interact with each other for the purpose of the show. "Daaamn baby, look at all that ass on you," DQ Dawg said as Sexy Duvall gave him a lap dance.

"You can't handle this!"

"I got ten stacks that says I can."

"You ain't the only one wit' money. Bet twenty that I'll have ya ass tappin' out in five minutes."

DQ Dawg's small entourage went wild hearing Sexy Duvall's response to his bet.

"We just gon' have to find out, ain't we?"

"Whatever!" Sexy Duvall said, walking away. As she did, money rained in the club.

"CUT!!" one of the producers yelled. The music stopped, and the lights came on in the club. "Good job, guys. Let's wrap this up." He signaled to the camera crew, twirling his hand in the air.

"You really think you can make me cum in five minutes?" DQ Dawg walked up to Sexy Duvall and asked her in her ear.

"All you gotta do is put ya twenty stacks up and see.

"Look, baby, I'll even let you cheat. I'll let you take whatever pill of ya choice, and still guarantee that ya ass'll cum in five!"

"Hey, sexy, I see you doin' ya reality TV thing. I was tryna get wit' you. I got whatever on it. Just name ya price," some random hustler said, cutting DQ Dawg and Sexy Duvall's conversation short.

"Go ahead and handle ya business. We gon' get together," DQ Dawg said.

"I think they got us shooting together a few mo' times, so I'll get ya info an' hit you so we can find out what we gon' do fo' the show," Sexy Duvall said to DQ Dawg.

"A'ight, sound 'bout right," DQ Dawg said, looking at Sexy Duvall, then at the small-time hustler who had cut his conversation with her short. Normally, he would have checked the disrespectful baller, but he didn't want the camera catching him being violent.

He was on parole, and didn't want to risk going to jail.

"So, what's up? Can I get'cha number? I'm tryna spend some money with you," the small-time baller said, watching DQ Dawg walk off.

"Yea, put my number in ya phone, and hit me up if you serious, and you ready to spend some real money. Don't hit me if you ain't gettin' money out here."

"Oh, I'm gettin' money. You'll see when I hit you

up," the small-time baller said as he put Sexy Duvall's number in his cell phone.

****

Meanwhile, at a different location, Blocks N Bricks was recording a studio session for *Love & Trap Muzik, Pittsburgh*.

"Lied to my man, said I was ten minutes away, but I'm at the spot whippin' a half of brick of yay/

Choppa on the table/

got two Pits at the door/

nina on my navel/

half of brick on the floor/

Bandana on my face!

I took a hammer to the cake!

Peruvian Flake/

it's that scaly white product!

Smashed it into powder/

heated that Visionware pot up."

As the recording engineer watched Blocks N Bricks spit his lyrics, he adjusted his vocal levels on the mixing board as the camera crew recorded the session.

"Let it cook a lil/

wit' that fire on medium/

grabbed the squirt gun/

and wit' the water/

started squeezin' it/

took a butter knife, and I slowly started whippin'/

in a couple minutes/

the cocaine started lookin' different/ went from a powder to a paste/ within seconds/

stripped down to my beater/ 'cause it's hot up, in the kitchen/ turned the fire off!

and I counter topped my weapon/ placed it in ice water!

and I watched it start to harden!

put it on paper towel/ to absorb the water/

let it dry a lil

and I weighed it on my scale/

called back some fiends

and said, I got this rock fo' sale/

called back my man

and told him I was on my way/

'cause this is how we do it in the cities of PA."

The engineer stopped the track, and played it back through the studio monitor's. "You like that?" Blocks N Bricks asked the engineer.

"You gon' have the streets sown up wit' that shit, straight up," the engineer said, bobbing his head to the track.

CHAPTER 7:

ALL MONEY AIN'T GOOD MONEY

Sexy Duvall screamed seductive profanities at one of her tricks that echoed off the walls of the DoubleTree Hotel. "Fuck me! Fuck me harder, daddy! Harder, daddy!"

Her John's dick was small, but his money was long. His baby-sized penis throbbed, covered in her pussy juices. Her John sweated as he tried to get his nut. He concentrated as Sexy Duvall instructed him, trying to save time. "Come on, baby. Cum, baby!" She wished he would hurry up and cum. All she wanted was his money.

Her client was Bradshaw Hemsley, an Allegheny County defense lawyer for the city of Pittsburgh. He had fought a case for her in 2011, and won, and she rewarded him by giving him a shot of head, and he had been turned out ever since.

Going down on her, Bradshaw placed Sexy Duvall's legs on his shoulders. Her pussy hairs were shaven clean, her clit protruded, hard and visible as it poked out. Bradshaw twirled circles around it with his tongue. Her pussy lips were firm and puffy, and they covered his mouth as his tongue stabbed in and out of her pussy hole.

"You muthafucka! You muthafucka! Make mommy cum! Make mommy cum!"

The least Bradshaw could do was make her cum, Sexy Duvall thought, palming his head, force-feeding him her dripping snatch. She wanted to have an orgasm, but she knew in order for her to get paid, she would have to make him cum also. She could have made Bradshaw cum within minutes, but she wanted him to feel as though he was getting his proper bang for his bucks.

"Oooh, shit! Shit, shit, shiiiit! Brad, I'm cummin'. I'm c-c-cummin'!" she moaned, fucking his tongue faster and harder as she came.

Grabbing Bradshaw, Sexy Duvall removed his face from her pussy. "Fuck my mouth. I wanna taste my pussy on ya dick. I wanna taste ya nut. Explode ya load in this hot, wet mouth of mine. I wanna swallow for you, daddy!"

Climbing aboard Sexy Duvall's face, Bradshaw guided his dick through Sexy Duvall's succulent lips, and slid his small man part in and out of her mouth, his balls slapped her chin repeatedly.

Sexy Duvall's medium sized hand gripped Bradshaw's ass cheeks, and her middle finger wiggled its way into his asshole.

"Yeeaah, do that. Do that, Sexy!" Bradshaw begged. As her manicured finger fingered his butt, her other hand clawed into the meat of his buttock. Bradshaw loved it. The faster he pumped and fucked her mouth, the more he moaned. Then his asshole clenched tight around her finger and Sexy Duvall knew that he was about to cum. "Oh, shit... Oh, shit, I'm cummin', Sexy. Baby, I'm cummin'!" Bradshaw exhaustedly said, pumping and thrusting his hips until they lost steam. His body clenched as he filled Sexy Duvall's

mouth with all the dick he could offer. Creamy, white cum shot into the walls of Sexy Duvall's mouth and she gulped and swallowed every bit of it.

"Mmm, Brad. That was so good, thick and delicious," Sexy Duvall said, wiping her face, and licking her fingers.

"Damn you," Bradshaw said after rolling off Sexy Duvall, and onto his back. "Oh, that was great, Sexy!"

Gathering her clothes, Sexy Duvall headed to the bathroom where she brushed her teeth, gargled and spit mouthwash into the toilet.

After rinsing her mouth out, she took

a shower, and thought about the reality TV show she was now a part of, and her conversation with DQ Dawg. Her itinerary said that the two of them were to be filming together the following day, and she made a mental note to call him and plan out what they would do on camera.

Sexy Duvall was a thirty-five-year-old stripper turned reality TV star. She had gained television popularity starring on *Bad Girls Club*, and now she was a part of the *Love & Trap Muzik, Pittsburgh* cast, starring opposite of local rapper, DQ Dawg, who was an up-and-coming rapper who had shot to the top of the charts with his single, “She Like It From The Baaack!"

Money King wanted the two of them to play a struggling couple striving for success on the show, but, of course, the choice was theirs. In reality, they didn't know each other, and they were both very successful. If they came up with an effective storyline, Money King told them that they would be offered a multiple-season contract.

Sexy Duvall and DQ Dawg had filmed once for the

show and had chemistry, so they would continue to pursue what Money King had suggested. They both wanted the multiple-season contract Money King had offered them, but until she got it, Sexy Duvall was still stripping and tricking in order to pay her bills.

As a good businesswoman, Sexy Duvall negotiated a deal that allowed her twenty-year old daughter, America Duvall, to star on a few episodes, and would make sure her daughter would cause enough controversy to gain a following of her own. Thanks to America and Sexy Duvall's strong social media following, they had both risen to ghetto-stardom. They both had close to two million followers on Instagram.

Before *Love & Trap Muzik, Pittsburgh*, Sexy Duvall made several thousand dollars a week. She was the highest paid exotic dancer in Pennsylvania, and was already being booked to host parties, so now she was averaging several thousand a night. Plus, she was selling pussy after her shows, and due to her newfound success, men and women

were willing to pay whatever her asking price was.

Walking out of the bathroom, she gazed at Bradshaw as he sat at the edge of the bed with an envelope in hand. "Same time next week?" he asked.

"If I'm not filming or don’t have any parties to host. I'll let you know early in the week," Sexy Duvall told Bradshaw.

"You know I need to see you at least once a week, darling."

"I know, daddy. I'll make something happen for you," Sexy Duvall said, giving Bradshaw a kiss.

"Here you go, doll," Bradshaw said, handing Sexy Duvall two thousand dollars.

"Thank you, Brad." She kissed Bradshaw again, adjusted her spandex dress, and walked her Red Bottoms out of the hotel door.

On the outside of the hotel, a light rain had started falling. Sexy Duvall trotted to her Aston Martin Vanquish with her cell phone glued to her ear. "I'm on my way," she said to another one of her clients. Inside her car, she looked at her cell phone screen as it blinked.

"Sexy Duvall," she answered. "What date? Okay, I'll let you know tomorrow," she said to someone trying to book her for a private party.

It was five A.M. by the time Sexy Duvall had finished with her third and final client. Physically exhausted, she couldn't wait to get home, take a shower, and get in her bed.

Rolling through Downtown Pittsburgh, her high-end rimmed wheels flicked water as they rotated. Rain was deflected by her windshield wipers as she looked out of it at the road ahead. Yellow, blinking traffic lights reflected off the wet streets as her metal horse galloped on the way to her palace.

The night had been good to her, and the pay was even better. She had cum at least six times, and had earned over ten thousand dollars.

The following week, she and her daughter, America, were being flown to New York by a record label executive. He was one of her favorite clients. He had agreed to a listening session, and if he liked what he heard, he promised to produce a hit for America.

Looking down at her cell phone as it rang, vibrated, and blinked, she picked it up, and examined the number of the caller. "Who the fuck is this?" she asked herself before answering.

"Sexy Duvall," she answered.

"Hey, Sexy. This is her, cah!" she heard the caller say to someone.

"Can I help you?" Sexy Duvall asked, wondering how the caller had gotten her number. She hoped that it was a serious inquiry, and not a groupie calling her business line. She had already changed her number twice in a week because of that.

"It's the dude you gave ya number to at Reflections the night you was doing that reality TV shit. You remember?" the caller said, trying to refresh her memory. Suddenly, she remembered the small-time hustler who had interrupted her conversation with DQ Dawg.

"What's up wit' you? I'm tryna holla!"

"Sorry, babe, I'm callin' it a night."

"Aw, don't go home. Come fuck wit' me. I'll make it worth ya while."

"If I turn my car around, it better be worth my while."

"Me and my man tryna fuck. I gotta stack fo' you," the caller said and paused, waiting for a response.

"BYE! You wastin' my time."

“Hol' up! Fifteen hunnid?" the caller negotiated.

"Twenty-five, nothin' less," Sexy Duvall relied.

The caller conversed with his friend and Sexy Duvall listened as he did. "A'ight, we got you. Where you wanna meet?"

"Meet me at Reflections, I'm by there now," Sexy Duvall said, referring to the strip club her manager, Dominican Flames, owned.

It had closed at 2:00 A.M., so they would have to meet in the parking lot.

"We're by there, too. See you in a couple minutes," the caller stated before hanging up.

Eight minutes had passed as Sexy Duvall watched as a car pulled into Reflection’s parking lot. Its headlights lit up her face as it pulled in, and parked in front of her car horizontally.

"What the fuck?" was all Sexy Duvall could say as she watched two armed men exit their car and approach hers with their gats drawn.

Fumbling through her purse, she searched for her .380. Seeing Sexy Duvall rambling through her purse made one of the jackers let three rounds go. *POP! POP! POP!*

Those three rounds filled Sexy Duvall's body, and

the last shot blew several locks of her micro-braids off, along with pieces of her flesh and skull.

"Yo! Nigga, what the fuck is you doin'?" the other jacker shouted. "We 'pose to be jackin' the bitch, not killin' her!" he added.

Sexy Duvall laid slumped to the side. Her body was stretched over the armrest and blood leaked through the bullet holes that burned through her flesh.

The small-time hustler who had shot Sexy Duvall used the butt of his Glock and smashed the driver-side window, causing glass to shatter on the ground and on Sexy Duvall's stiff body.

"Nigga, shut the fuck up fo' I shoot ya ass, too!" the shooter said, unlocking Sexy Duvall's car doors. "Go to the other side and pop the trunk," he told the other jacker.

When the small-time hustler opened the car door, Sexy Duvall let off two shots through her purse, and her slugs blasted through the shooter's face and chest. She struck him with two deadly blows; once in the forehead, and once in the center of his pecs. The impact from Sexy Duvall's .380 forced the would-be jacker backward.

POP! He managed to release his final shot into the air before stumbling backward, and collapsing to his demise.

Uncertain of what had transpired, the other jacker panicked, and ran for his car. But as he tried to pull away, Sexy Duvall pulled her shift into drive and crashed into the side of the jacker's car, and made him fishtail as he fled from the scene.

Sexy Duvall's foot abruptly stopped her car and she managed to put it in park. "Fuck! Agh!" She gasped for air as the bullet holes in her body leaked more crimson fluid. Using all her strength, she reached for her cell

phone. In extreme pain, she managed to dial 911. "Hellllp! Helllp," were the final words she spoke before passing out.

After receiving the news about her mother being shot, America Duvall, Sexy Duvall's twenty-year-old daughter, collapsed to the floor and screamed. Then she received another call that hurt her more. "Your grandmother heard about your mother and had a heart attack. She's being rushed to Allegheny General," the caller said. Now she had to deal with two tragedies.

Putting her hands to her face, she broke into a million pieces. She couldn't gather herself. America screamed again and again, only calming down when she saw Money King's name on the LCD screen of her cell phone.

"Money! Money!" she answered.

"America, try to calm yourself, baby. Everything's gonna

be a'ight. I'm on my way to the hospital. I'll meet you there. We'll talk once you get there," Money King told the hysterical America Duvall.

"Okay. That's my brother on the other line. I have to answer it," America said, clicking over to answer her brother's call.

Renault "Ren" Duvall was America's older brother. Word of his mother being shot had also gotten to him.

"Sis, I'll be there in five minutes. What the fuck happened?" he asked, yelling into his cell phone.

"I don't know. All I know is Ma got shot at Reflections, and Grandma had a heart attack!"

"Grandma had a heart attack? Oh my God! Fuuuccck! This shit's crazy, man. I'll be there." *Click*.

Pacing back and forth, America quickly grew impatient as she waited for Ren. "What am I gon' do without them? What am I gonna do?" she questioned herself. Feeling confused, she grabbed her purse and headed out the door. At the same time, Ren was calling her phone. He was outside.

CHAPTER 8:

LET DOWNS & COME UPS

At Clun Reflection, Dominican Flames and her security were in her office. She was on her way back from Philly when her client, Sexy Duvall, had gotten shot. When she got back to Pittsburgh, she called a meeting with her security and street goons. She had flipped after hearing that the head of her security team had given the security camera footage of the shooting to the police.

“What the fuck you mean you don't have the footage? What the fuck do you mean you gave the footage to the police, muthafucka? I got TMZ calling me, offering me a hunnid bands, and you just gave the shit away?" Dominican Flames yelled at the head of her security.

"I didn't know," the security guard said, trying to defend his actions.

"You didn't know? What? Are you stupid? Huh, muthafucka? Are you stupid? Man, get the fuck outta my face!" Dominican Flames said, dismissing him.

"Come on, Dom," the security guard pleaded for reason.

"Get outta my face! Go find some'in' to do while I figure shit out. I'll call ya ass when I'm ready fo' ya ass to come back. No! Matter of fact, go get that nigga’s blood outta my parking lot. That's what ya dumb ass could do. Yea, go do that, and think about that blood being ya blood because, one day soon, ya blood could be getting cleaned up. That's how hot I am right now."

"Dom, they said it was fo' their investigation," the security guard said, standing his ground.

"I don't give a fuck! You don't release shit without my permission. Did they have a warrant?

"You better get outta here fo' we have a real problem, seriously," Dominican Flames told the head of her security team, standing amongst her other security guards and street goons. Her blood was boiling, and she was getting angrier by the second.

What she didn't know was the security guard was only acting stupid. He had made plans to sell a copy of the footage to TMZ himself, but when America Duvall had called and offered him seventy-five bands for it, he accepted her deal. So, actually, he had outsmarted Dominican Flames. He had made two copies of the footage; one, he gave to the police, and the other, he made a profit from, but he would soon find out that she was the wrong boss bitch to play.

Greed had gotten the best of the security guard. Even he knew that he was risking his life by deceiving Dominican Flames, but he was counting on her never finding out that he had betrayed her.

Dominica “Dominican Flames” Duarte was the princess of two well connected Dominican crack lords, Giselle “El Grunona” Duarte and Peter “Brooklyn Pete” Duarte. They both had twenty-one years in on their life sentences. They had put in for clemency several times, and had been denied time after time, but they weren't giving up.

With Congressional attempts to restore sentencing

discretilon judges, and the fairness in the Cocaine Sentencing Act in 2009, thousands of crack dealers had received some relief. Unfortunately, they didn't because of their life sentences. When the bill abolished the heightened penalties and mandatory minimums for drug offenses involving cocaine-base such as crack cocaine, they both believed that they would be immediately released, but that wasn't the case. Now their only chance at freedom would have to come through President Obama. It had been rumored that within his last months in office, he would grant inmates such as them clemency.

Upon hearing about the Duvall family tragedy, Dominican Flames' parents had called to give their condolences. Dominican Flames and America Duvall had grown up calling one another sisters. America's grandmother and mother worked for Dominican Flames' parents, and she even dated America's brother, Ren, up until their grandmother's indictment.

Around nine a.m. the next morning, DQ Dawg and his man 2 Gatz discussed Sexy Duvall's shooting at his home in North Hills. "Shit's crazy, fam. I couldn't even sleep a wink last night, dawg. All I could do was think about Sexy being shot. I know I don't really know her, but I'm really feeling her, you know?" DQ Dawg said to 2 Gatz.

"Shit, nigga, just imagine if she would've gave you a shot of that head she was tellin' ya ass about," 2 Gatz said, making light of the situation.

"Nigga, shut the fuck up!"

"They say she clapped back and killed one of them boys, tho'."

"Hell yea. She's a G fo' that. She's gangsta as hell. I'm really feeling that bitch."

"Did you try to go see her?"

"Yea, but they're only lettin' her immediate family see her. They say her mom died of a heart attack after hearing that she had been shot."

"That shit's fucked up."

"Hell yea."

DQ Dawg's cell phone vibrated. "It's the producer of the show," DQ Dawg said, picking his phone up and screening the call.

"Yo!" he answered. "Okay, okay, I'm on it. Cool." The producer of the show had told him to check his email.

Being that Sexy Duvall had gotten shot, they had switched up the events on his itinerary. They had also told him to promote the *Love & Trap Muzik, Pittsburgh*'s web page, and to tell his five hundred thousand followers to check out the site that following Tuesday night. That was when they would be advertising their first season.

"Oh, that's what's up. You know you gotta drop a video fo' Sexy and her moms," 2 Gatz said.

"Hell yea. That's the craziest shit I ever heard," DQ Dawg said, checking his email.

"What they got planned fo' you?" 2 Gatz asked.

"They tryna put me and that boy Blocks N Bricks in the same spot at the same time. I guess they wanna see some drama," DQ Dawg said with a chuckle.

"Oh, they definitely gon' see some if they do that. How the fuck they don't know y'all rap rivals? Them people got some shit wit' them."

"Yo, they know. Shit, who don't know that? Our beef is all over the internet, and you know they need that kinda beef fo' the show. That's what these reality shows are made of: drama!" DQ Dawg muttered. Like Mr. Frosty Blow and Smack Down, Blocks N Bricks and DQ Dawg were once partners. But after a dispute over royalties, they split up, and soon after became rivals, and battled for rap supremacy.

****

At the Hyatt Hotel, across town, Blocks N Bricks was beating a THOT's pussy up. "Whose pussy is this? Whose pussy is this?"

"Blocks N Bricks! Blocks N Bricks." It sounded like he was laying one of his tracks. The groans and moans from the morning session were rhythmic. Feeling himself about to cum, he pulled out and jacked off until he shot cum up her abdomen.

"Why you pull out? Fuck! I was about to cum," the THOT said.

Blocks N Bricks' cell phone sounded and vibrated.

"Don't answer that. Give me some mo' dick. Please, bae," the THOT begged.

"Bitch, is you crazy? This might be some money," he said.

"Hello? Okay. Huh? Now y'all know I don't fuck wit' that bitch-ass nigga. A'ight, thanks."

"Who was that?" the THOT asked, grabbing Blocks N Bricks.

"Why is you all in my business? Damn! That was the producer of the show. They got me filming wit' that bitch-ass nigga DQ Dawg, and they know I don't fuck wit' him."

"You gotta do what you gotta do. Plus, that's mo' money in the bank fo' us."

"What? Bitch, you crazy! What you mean mo' money fo' us? You ain't help me write my raps!"

"Whatever! Come on, let's finish. I'm tryna cum."

"See, that's ya problem. Ya young, dumb and full of cum. All you wanna do is smoke and fuck. That's why I ain't puttin' ya ass on the show."

" Why?" the THOT asked, sucking her teeth.

"'Cause ya all about a fuck, and I'm all about a buck. So, besides fucking, we ain't got shit in common."

After the producer of *Love & Trap Muzik, Pittsburgh* had called him, Blocks N Bricks felt the pressure. He knew that he was up against stiff competition, and to make an impact on the show, he knew he would have to dig deep into himself and pull out the best he had to offer the world. He didn't like DQ Dawg, but he couldn't deny that he was very talented as a rapper. Besides that, every club he went to was playing his new single, *She Like It From The Baaack*!

Unlike the other artists on the show, he had big shoes to fill. His father was a rap legend, and expected him to always be on top of his game. In order to run the baton and win the first-place medallion, Blocks N Bricks knew that he would have to find a balance between underground battle rap and mainstream success like his father had.

CHAPTER 9:

WHAT'S THE DEAL

Monte Bucks called America and asked to meet with her. The meeting would be filmed for the show at a restaurant that overlooked the city of Pittsburgh.

When America pulled up to Pittsburgh's premier Mt. Washington Oyster House, she saw the *Love & Trap Muzik* security team and camera crew on set, and readied herself. She checked her face in her visor mirror and did a slight makeup touch up. After being prompted and being mic'd up, she entered the restaurant where Love & Trap Muzik's financier, Monte Bucks, sat patiently waiting.

ACT ONE SCENE A

For this particular shot, the producers had bought out a section of the dining area, and had placed actors at surrounding tables in place of real patrons to make the background look authentic and natural.

As America took her seat, an African American, full figured female waitress approached the dining table on cue, and placed water and menus down on the table.

"I'll give you guys a few minutes to decide," the waitress

said, doing as she was scripted to do. She was also a paid actress.

Before shooting began, America was told that she could order food, but they were just going to be filming for the duration of the shoot. So, after ordering, the colloquy between America and Monte Bucks evoked.

"First of all, thank you for meeting me, America. I'm...," Monte Bucks began to say, and paused. "Sorry about what happened to your grandmother and mother. What a tragedy, and like I said on the phone, I'll be taking care of all expenses, so don't worry about that," Monte Bucks said, hoping to ease any financial worries.

"Thank you so much, Mr. Bucks. Thank you."

"No, call me Monte, and you don't need to thank me. But, uh, getting straight down to business, I believe that I can put a great opportunity on the table for you."

"Um, okay. A great opportunity?"

"Look, here's the deal. I would like for you to fill in for your mother. I'll have my people draw up your contract, and we can go over it, but like I said, I believe that this is a great opportunity for you to promote your music, and to speak out against violence," Monte Bucks said, watching America ponder what he was saying.

"It does sound like a great opportunity, I must admit." "Hey, we've already started shooting season one. You've already been introduced to our audience through your mother, and now with what has happened, we feel—and I don't mean any disrespect—your mother being shot and the upcoming funeral will be just what we need to draw in a massive amount of followers, and boost our ratings along the way. This would bring a *The First 48* twist to a Hip Hop reality show, something that has never been done before. We could keep up with the investigation, and we're currently trying to work out a deal with the Pittsburgh Police force to get the interrogation tapes and the surveillance footage before TMZ gets their hands on it. So, what do you say?" Monte said, patiently waiting for a response as America's eyes wandered absently around the restaurant.

"We have to move fast," Monte Bucks added.

“You talk about ratings, Mr. Bucks, but this is a very serious matter to me and my family, and if I do this, I know I'ma receive a lot of backlash from the blogs and social media."

"That's what we want; we want social media involved. And, as far as your family, with the amount of money I'm going to pay you, I'm pretty sure they'll understand.

“Look, this is an opportunity of a lifetime for you, for me, and for your moms. You say you wanna be a star; well, this is the kind of move that could make you a mega star."

"True. And you say that the payoff is going to be...?"

"Six figures. You'll be the highest paid cast member on the show. Plus, everything will revolve around you and your family." Stroking his salt-and-pepper goatee, he waited for her response.

"Six figures? That could be a hunnid thousand," America said, shrugging her shoulders.

"Or nine hundred thousand."

"Make it seven figures, and I'll throw in the footage," America countered.

"Footage?" Monte Bucks repeated, stretching his neck, and bending his ear towards America as if to hear her clearer.

"Yea, I got the footage. There's two copies; I got one, and the police got the other one. But the difference between my copy and their copy is I have the full copy, so what you wanna do? TMZ is offering six figures, and I ain't talking about the low end."

"Bullshit!"

"Mr. Bucks—"

"Monte, call me Monte."

"Okay. Well, Monte, I wouldn't bullshit you. Now, being that you want to record the funeral, burial and all—that is what you wanna do, isn't it?"

"Yea. That's what I wanna do."

"Then I know you know that time is of the essence. So, using your words, we gotta move fast."

Monte laughed. He was impressed with America's business savvy.

"So, do we have a deal?" America asked, pulling out her cell phone, and sitting it on the table.

"What's that, the footage?" Monte asked, reaching for the phone, and America let him take it.

"Yup, but like I said, if you wanna capitalize off this great opportunity, as you called it, then we have to make a deal now and get this footage out somehow."

Monte nodded his head in agreement, and pressed play on the cell phone, and the video started uploading. *POP! POP! POP!* Sexy Duvall's gun popped, and the jacker who had opened her door was blown away.

"Daaammmn!" Monte Bucks exclaimed, loudly, not believing what he had seen.

"So, do we have a deal?"

"You know what? I underestimated you. You're a good businesswoman, even better than your mother. The world's going to love you. A million dollars it is," Monte Bucks said, taking a sip of his water. He knew that what he was looking at was worth ten times as much. "I'll have my people write everything up, and you'll have a million dollars within the hour," Monte Bucks said, still watching the footage.

"No problem, it's yours," America said, pushing back from the table.

"This is what I'm going to do. I'ma have my people whip together a promo commercial, and we'll all just push it through our social media platforms."

"We're going to have to do it quick so we can get this footage out before anybody else."

"Oh, I'm tryna do this within the next few days. I got some of the best editors in the game, and I'm going to book some of the best artists in the game. We gon' blow this shit up, lil mama!"

"It sounds like it."

"Hey, tho', one question..."

What up?"

"How did you get the footage? Did Dominican Flames give it to you?"

"Nah, my people got it fo' me."

CHAPTER 10:

COPS, THOTS, & BALLAS

Smack Down sat up in bed at a THOT's Northside home, and thought about what he had to do on that particular day. He was thinking about making two, no more than three more drug transactions before getting out of the game. It had been three days since he had spoken to his connect. The night before had gotten the best of him, and he sent his connect a text message before he had fallen asleep, but got no response. He figured his connect was still in motion, so that didn't bother him. If anything ever went wrong, his connect's lawyer would contact him, and that wasn't the case, so he knew that everything was good.

There had been times that he had waited up to two weeks for his drugs to be delivered. He wasn't a small-time corner boy anymore. His drug purchases took time to be paid for, processed, packaged and shipped, so he knew that it was just a matter of time. Bored the night before, he went to Reflection and left with a THOT and her stripper friend.

After a few moments of contemplating, the vibrations and alert of his cell phone brought Smack Down out of his trance. Checking his text messages, he smiled. He had several text messages, but the first one was from his connect.

He was told to meet him five days from the date. The meeting spot was predetermined, and the money had already been exchanged. All Smack Down had to do was pick up his work. Normally, it was just as easy as that, but lately, he had the *Love & Trap Muzik, Pittsburgh*'s camera crew following him, so he would have to get rid of them before he could go pick up his work. Scrolling down, he checked his second message. It was from the producers of the show.

TEXT MESSAGE (TWO):

LOVE & TRAP MUZIK, PITTSBURGH TEASER PARTY this Friday 9:00 P.M.- 2:00 A.M.

The producers had sent out an email-burst and text messages to the cast members and V.I.P., inviting them to attend a party that would reveal the trailer for the show. Smack Down grunted, thinking that he only had two days to prepare. Then he scrolled down to his third message; it was from Money.

TEXT MESSAGE (THREE):

Where the fuck are you? I'm getting tired of your shit!!!

WE TRAP OR DIE 89

After erasing his connect's message, Smack Down sat his cell phone on the bedroom lampstand, and looked over at the two women he'd had a threesome with the night before. Cinnamon was Cuban and Labanese, 34C-26-36, and was from Brick City, New Jersey. Suga was Italian and Irish, 34B-27-46, and she was from Harlem, New York. They both worked at Reflection; Cinnamon was a barmaid and Suga was a dancer. They worked as a team, playing, using, seducing and luring men to bed for large fees.

Smack Down grabbed Cinnamon's ass and shook

her. "Hm?" she groaned. Smack Down shook her again, and she groaned again, "Hm?" This time, she turned and looked at him with one eye open, her head resting on her folded arms. She knew what he wanted, but she was still tired from the night before.

Smack Down felt Cinnamon's hand climb up his leg, and take hold of his manhood underneath the covers. "You know what time it is," Smack Down blurted out. Thinking of Cinnamon's nipple and clit piercings helped his dick stay hard.

"Stay in that position, don't move!" the cameraman told the three show participants. The show had been recording them since the night before. They had stopped recording before the action started, and were back to capture the morning after footage. "Okay. CUT!" The cameraman cut the scene, and the camera crew packed up and left.

Once Cinnamon let the camera crew out of her house, she got back in bed with her two lovers. "Now I want some dick," she told Smack Down as she stroked his man piece. As his ass cheeks clenched, his dick grew more and more.

Reaching over, Smack Down cupped and squeezed her expensive tits. "Oooh," Cinnamon moaned. Going down on him, she held his erect dick and swiped her tongue back and forth over his dick head before taking him into her mouth. The warmth and wetness of her mouth caused Smack Down's eyes roll to the back of his head as Cinnamon's head jerked up and down on his dick. She liked the way his pre-cum tasted, and loved swallowing his sweet, savory cum.

Awakened by the sounds of morning sex, Suga joined in by kissing Smack Down, and grabbing Cinnamon by the ass. "Put that ass in the air, bitch!" Suga said to Cinnamon, and she tooted her ass up to be eaten. Suga spread her ass cheeks and stuck her tongue in Cinnamon's asshole as far as she could.

Cinnamon parted her lips and poured saliva onto Smack Down's dick like syrup on a breakfast sausage, then she ate all she could eat.

"Yes, yes, eat that ass, bitch!" Cinnamon looked back and told Suga as she tongue-fucked her asshole, and her fingers slipped in and out of her slippery cunt.

"Oh, baby. Oh, baby... Eat me, EAT ME!" Cinnamon managed to get out with a mouth full of thick, pulsating meat pumping in and out of her throat.

Grabbing Cinnamon by a fist full of her weave at the back of her head, Smack Down pulled her up from his dick. He crawled back from her, trying to escape submission, but her mouth sought after his cum-shooter like a fugitive on the run.

"Un-un, papi. You gon' cum in this mouth," Cinnamon said.

"Oooh... Mmm, shit!" Hearing her say that made him cum. "F-f-fuuuccck yes! Yes!" Hearing Smack Down cumming, Suga helped Cinnamon suck cum from his dick, and licked the white glaze that ran down between his legs and balls. "Fffuuucck!" Smack Down couldn't handle the tingling sensation the cum-thirsty THOT's caused his body to feel.

"Whoa! Y'all some nasty bitches, and I love it," Smack Down said as the two women posted up on his chest with smiles on their faces.

****

Inside his office, at the head of the squad room, bureau commander, Lieutenant Percy Combs, had been browsing the internet for thirty minutes. He finger-swiped through files and footage, looking for clues that would lead him to the second suspect in Case #1220, the Sexy Duvall case.

Setting his iPad down, he took out a cigarette from a pack that sat on his desk, and lit it, never taking his eyes off Sexy Duvall's Facebook profile picture. He exhaled cigarette smoke into the air before resting his cancer stick in an ashtray. Checking her post, he stopped at a digital copy of a flyer promoting the *Love & Trap Muzik, Pittsburgh* Teaser Party. Clicking on the comments, he noticed most of them were get well messages, prayers and condolences attached to prayer hand pictures, or blue skies and doves. Swiping downward, he came to a post of pictures of Sexy Duvall with celebrities at parties she had hosted. Opening another window on his iPad, he Googled the *Love & Trap Muzik, Pittsburgh* cast members, and noticed another female with the same last name as Sexy Duvall. So, he searched her name on Facebook and learned that America Duvall was Sexy Duvall's daughter. Pressing play on a link on her page titled, *SEXY DUVALL GOES IN*.

Lt. Combs picked up his cancer stick, took a pull, and exhaled from his nose as he watched America film her mother pole dancing at Reflection.

"THIS IS AMERICA DUVALL, BITCHES! I WANT Y'ALL TO SEE HOW WE GET THIS MONEY," America said, turning her cell phone camera to her mother as she worked the pole.

"I need to get me some pussy," Lt. Combs said, tugging at his crotch, fighting his erection as he watched Sexy Duvall's exotic dance.

Knock, knock, knock!

"You wanna see us Lt.?" robbery-homicide detective, Castaneda Gordy, asked. Behind her was her partner, Detective Ray Burnam. They stood in the entrance of the office, waiting for Lt. Combs to respond.

"Which one of y'all would like to explain this?" Lt. Combs asked, laying his iPad down in front of the detectives to view.

Standing up, he took another pull of his cigarette that was burning close to the butt. Waiting for an answer, he smashed it into his ashtray. "I take it you muthafuckas ain't surprised about the leak, so explain the shit! How in the fuck did TMZ get their hands on our evidence, and how did it get all over the internet?" Lt. Combs asked in a harsher voice, gazing angrily at the two investigators for what seemed to be an eternity. The expression on his face was a cross between disappointment and displeasure.

Somehow, the footage of the Sexy Duvall shooting had leaked, and made its way over to TMZ. The leak confirmed to many the patterns governing the corrupt police department of Pittsburgh. Knowing that they were guilty of the leakage, neither of the detectives said a word at first. They were willing to stand up for one another, and go down together.

"You two have been bringing a lot of heat on this department lately. This is the last time." Lt. Combs paused, looking both of the detectives in the eyes. "The last fuckin' time I'ma warn y'all asses. Next time y'all assholes' names come across this desk, y'all gon' be pushing pens like a muthafuckin' baker. You understand me?"

"Lt...." Taking in all the critical backlash she could take, Detective Gordy tried to explain their position. The two detectives were even willing to give the lieutenant a percentage of the fifty thousand dollars they had made from the footage, but Lt. Combs wouldn't allow her to get a full sentence out. "But, Lt.—"

"Oh, no you don't! You don't get to talk ya way outta this one, so don't even try to run ya bullshit on me, Castaneda. I know how hard it is to fight the temptations out there, how hard it is to make a couple extra dollars; believe me, I've been there. I know the pay cuts and the cut back on extra hours got y'all in a tight spot. I've been doing this for thirty years, so I know what's up, but I know that y'all don't want Internal Affairs breathing down y'all's necks again, making y'all's lives a living hell for the third time, now do you?" Lt. Combs asked, getting close to Detective Ray Barnum. His breath smelled of coffee and cigarettes.

"Lt.," Detective Gordy said, tired of hearing the lieutenant's mouth.

"WHAT, CASTANEDA?"

"We've identified the second suspect in the Sexy Duvall case," Detective Gordy said. Her statement made the room go silent for a brief moment.

"You've ID'd him?" Lt. Combs asked, taking his seat, and leaning back in it. "You guys have saved y'all's asses once again 'cause y'all was definitely close to being suspended," Lt. Combs said, accepting a manila envelope from Detective Burnam. "So, this is our guy, huh? Andrew Kaus?" he questioned, feeling relieved.

The pressure from the Stop The Violence groups in Pittsburgh was causing a lot of tension because, not only did Sexy Duvall get shot three times, but her mother had died of a massive heart attack after hearing about the shooting. The violence was personally effecting the community, so the level of frustration was increasing by the day.

Prior to this investigative report, their leads had been questionable, and not convicting. The investigation had come to a screeching halt after the first forty-eight hours. They had a partial license plate number, but were unable to find the owner of the getaway car.

As Lt. Combs looked over the evidence, a smile stretched across his face.

"Thanks to the high quality of the video, Cylabs was able to use modern facial recognition software to generate sixty to seventy pixels between the suspects eyes and apply super-resolution algorithm to the image to extrapolate what the suspect looked like straight on," Detective Gordy explained.

"Mm-hm." Lt. Combs shook his head with approval of the investigative technique used to identify the suspect.

"Then we posted the image online, and within thirty minutes, leads started pouring in," Detective Burnam added.

The software they spoke about was created by Mario Svvides, Head of Carnegie Mellon's Cylab. Using his software, they were able to generate a 3D version of the suspect's face from a 2D image, then they got the public involved using social media to do the rest of the work.

"This is excellent work. Excellent work, guys. Have we located the suspect yet?" Lt. Combs asked.

"We're pursuing a few leads."

"Well, for Christ sakes, what the hell are you guys still standin' here for? Go get this muthafucka off the streets!" Lt. Combs said, proud of the two corrupt detectives.

CHAPTER 11:

COPS, THOTS, & BALLAS II

CRIMINAL COMPLAINT: Case #1220

After a three-hour standoff in the Lawrenceville section of Pittsburgh, SWAT officers entered a house on 28th St., and arrested Andrew Kaus, twenty-six, of Wilkinsburg, PA after receiving a tip that the suspect was there. Kaus was charged with the robbery and shooting of reality TV star, Sexy Duvall. Kaus' accomplice, Brian Clurman, twenty-two, was shot and killed by Duvall during the crime.

Kaus accused his deceased partner of planning the robbery and shooting Duvall. Congruent to the police reports, Kaus was charged with homicide, robbery, conspiracy and firearm violations. According to court paperwork, the two men discussed robbing Duvall after witnessing her make a substantial amount of money dancing at Reflections nightclub. Kaus called Duvall in expectations that they were to have sex for money.

Cell phone records indicated that the last call Duvall received came from Kaus' cell phone, which was later found on his person at the time of his arrest.

During interviews with Allegheny County robbery detectives, Kaus said that Clurman shot Duvall multiple times, and after witnessing his accomplice, Clurman, get shot and killed, Kaus said he got scared and fled the scene, but not before his car was struck by the shooting victim, Sexy Duvall.

His statement was reconfirmed by surveillance footage and forensic evidence, which shows that on Thursday, April 7, 2016, the two co-conspirators pulled in front of Duvall's car, blocking her exit. The two men then stepped from the shadows of their car with their weapons drawn. At extreme close range, Clurman aimed his pistol at Sexy Duvall, who sat behind the steering wheel of her Aston Martin

Vanquish and shot into the windshield, hitting Duvall multiple times. Duvall was struck in the face, neck, chest, leg and abdomen. Slumped over in her seat, her body riddled with bullets, Duvall waited for the shooter to open her door in an attempt to rob her, and when he did, Duvall returned fire. Shooting through her Birkin bag, she hit the assailant twice, making him stumble backward, collapse and die. As the second assailant tried to get away, Duvall found the strength to ram his vehicle in an attempt to stop him from escaping.

A quarter of a block away, the gunfire and the car crash was heard by a pedestrian who happened to be driving by at the time the crime was being committed. Minutes later, his eyes met those of the fleeing suspect, Andrew Kaus. Focusing on the license plate of the wrecked Dodge Charger that abruptly pulled out in front of him, he thumbed part of the license plate into his smart phone. Seeing the direction, the suspect had come from,

the pedestrian dialed 911 and headed to where he believed the crime had been committed. After driving for approximately thirty seconds, he came upon a woman, later identified as Sexy Duvall, lying in the street, several feet from her car, the court documents said.

Kaus was arraigned Wednesday, April 13, 2016, and is being held at the Allegheny County Jail.

"It's a miracle that she's alive," Monte Bucks said after reading over the report he had requested.

He sat with the other producers of the show, discussing the edits and information that would be used to create the teaser commercial.

"What are they doing with her?" he asked about Sexy Duvall, adjusting himself in the leather seat of his home theater.

"She's being charged with a firearm violation because the gun she had was stolen, but they dropped the manslaughter charge after reviewing the tape."

"Okay, what about bail?"

"The bail situation is difficult because of her condition. They can't remove her from the hospital bed, but eventually, she will be arraigned, and that's when we'll know how much they want for bail. Until then, she's being heavily guarded. You saw how much red tape we had to go through to get footage for the teaser."

"Regardless of what her bail is, I want her out. Listen,

call my lawyer and have him contact the judge to do a bail hearing without her, and get her released on bail."

"That'll leave her unguarded at the hospital. The second suspect got arrested, but that don't mean he doesn't have goons. They might still try to get at her."

"Then hire twenty-four-hour security. Get her ass on camera for the show. I'm not paying her all that money for nothing. We need access to her as well as her daughter."

****

Scheduled to record for the show, Mr. Frosty Blow made his way to Platinum Beats, a studio owned by the super-producer, Boom-Bap.

He had an appointment with her that would be recorded for the show, but recording a reality show and living a reality show meant two different things. So, on his way to the recording studio, Mr. Frosty Blow kept his head on swivel. He kept his eyes open for any drama that life might bring him. He knew that in the city of Pittsburgh, anything could jump off, whether they were recording or not. It was scripted for him to meet up with the super-producer, but he stayed ready for the unscripted to happen.

Driving through the city, he got a lot of attention because of the car he was driving, and he knew somewhere in the crowd of onlookers, jealousy and jackers were lurking. Platinum records, money, jewelry and cars were attractions that could lead to trouble, sometimes even death, and he possessed them all. But, Mr. Frosty Blow was a real street nigga who came from the hood, and had put in work growing up in the hood. The street elements of the city knew this, so whenever he bought out his toys, jackers thought twice about trying him. He wasn't the type of rapper just rapping about shit he didn't live; he lived what he rapped about, so anyone stepping up to test him knew that there would be consequences and repercussions for fucking with his.

Unlike his rival, Smack Down, he rarely traveled in a pack unless he was traveling with his show entourage. Wherever he was, he carried his licensed FN Herstal 5.7 tactical strap. It held twenty in the clip, one in the chamber, fired high-velocity rounds, and penetrated bulletproof vests.

Earlier that day, he had purchased a red Lambo truck for the teaser party, but at this time, he rode in his '73 Chevy Caprice Donk on 10.5-inch wide wheels. Its engine was transformed into a 632ci BBC dyno-ed at 905hp on pump gas with no power adders or nitrous. It was the most powerful heart you could put in a Donk. Everything about his Caprice said money; even his break system cost him over eight stacks.

Platinum Beats was located on the twenty fifth floor of PNC Plaza, a condo building in Downtown Pittsburgh's hottest new district adjacent to the thriving new development of Market Square, and a burgeoning retail and restaurant scene. The duplex penthouses' six bedrooms were converted into Studio Room's A, B, C, D, E and F. Its original structural columns and beam ceilings sprawled across 4,500-square feet on two levels with more than 3,000 square-feet of open loft living that served as an outdoor dining area complete with waiters and barmaids. A cantilevered solid oak and steel staircase called Boom Bap's Ladder ascended to the twenty sixth floor, or as Boom Bap called it, Heaven, and everything was white. Floor to ceiling windows slid open to a roomy terrace with a stone patio and hot tub.

On this day, Boom Bap's sessions were running

close. At the last moment, she had decided to squeeze a client in between her meeting with Mr. Frosty Blow. Both were being filmed for the show.

Boom Bap was a forty-year-old, bi-sexual who had a thing for younger men and women between the ages of twenty and twenty-five years old. The real reason she was mad at producer, Making Hitz, wasn't because he had gone into business for himself—she was really proud of him for that—it was because he had stopped fucking her. She was looking forward to seeing him at the teaser party, and hoped that they could reconcile their differences.

As Boom Bap and her client wrapped up their listening session, Mr. Frosty Blow made his way through the lobby of Platinum Beats Studio, and asked the receptionist to let Boom Bap and the camera crew know that he was there. "Okay, I'll let them know," the receptionist told him as he took a seat on one of the plush chairs in the lobby, looking out the wall of windows permitting a panoramic scene of Downtown Pittsburgh. Instead of magazines, iPads were made available in the waiting area. At one swipe of your finger, you could access any book or magazine of your preference.

As Mr. Frosty Blow looked out at the people walking through Market Square, the camera crew began to walk into the lobby. Without hesitation, they mic'd him up, and readied him for filming.

Inside Studio Room A, Boom Bap's cell phone vibrated. "Okay. Great." Her receptionist let her know that Mr. Frosty Blow was headed up to the studio. "That's my other client. He's on his way up. Just check out the beats, write to 'em, get a feel for 'em, and let me know which ones you want."

“A’ight, that sounds good," Boom Bap's client said with her hand on the doorknob. She felt it twist and saw Mr. Frosty Blow enter the studio.

"Yo, Boom Bap! Oh, shit! What up, America? I didn’t know you was up here," he said, entering the studio.

"Yea, checking out some tracks for my new mixtape," America told Mr. Frosty Blow. The two reality stars had met through America's mom at Reflections months before the show had gotten the green light. When he got the email that she would be joining the cast, Mr. Frosty Blow was happy for her.

"Sorry to hear about what happened, yo. You comin' to the teaser party Friday?"

"Hell yea. You know I'ma be front and center."

"That's what's up. Where you goin', tho’? You might as well chill. We might can come up wit' some'in'."

"A collabo wit' y'all two would be dope as shit, and we could premiere it at the teaser party," Boom Bap added.

"What you think, ma?" Mr. Frosty Blow asked America.

"I'm wit' it. I need ya platinum touch to rub off on me," America said with a smile on her face.

CHAPTER 12:

ACT OF WAR

At a trap house on the west side of Pittsburgh, Hitter B., Smack Down's street goon and producer/engineer said, "Smack, check this bitch out," showing him an Instagram video of America and Mr. Frosty Blow recording at Platinum Beats.

"At Platinum Beats Studio wit' two legends; platinum beat maker, Boom Bap, and the owner of Pittsburgh's streets, Mr. Frosty Blow!" America said, streaming a video from her iPhone.

"Get the fuck outta here. That nigga don't own the streets, we do! Bitch crazy!" Smack Down replied, tight about the title America had given his friend turned foe.

"Bruh, it's time to put that lame in his place, and we need to jack that bitch to get her straight, you know? I could take her out to our new spot, and make her tell us where all the guap is," Hitter B. said, trying to convince Smack Down to check Mr. Frosty Blow, and kidnap America.

"Be easy, homie. They down there on camera. But we gon' go holla at that nigga, tho'. I'm tired of that muthafucka actin' like he own shit. This my muthafuckin' city, our muthafuckin' city!"

"You fuckin' right it is, Smack!" Hitter B. said, and the rest of his bobble headed goons chimed in and bobbed their heads in agreement.

"Y'all niggas stay here and get this work together.

Me and Hitter gon' go holla at that nigga. Break these four birds down in quarter bricks, double these three, and put these three up," Smack Down barked orders at the Smack Dizzy Boyz as he took his Walther PPX .40 Caliber out of his waistband, ejected the clip, examined it to make sure it was fully loaded, inserted it back in, slid the slide back, loading one in the chamber, and put it back in his waistband.

"Yo, fam', don't go down there doin' shit on camera. Smack, man, we got a lot ridin' on you. You don't need no case right now," Smack Down's second in charge, Cash, told him.

"Nigga, shut the fuck up wit' that scared shit. That nigga out there disrespectin' the squad, and ya ass scared to catch a case," Hitter B. said to Cash.

"Nigga, you shut the fuck up!" Cash said, standing up, ready to rumble if he had to.

"Man, fall back wit' all that bullshit. We all on the same team here. Cash, you're right; we can't afford to get indicted on drugs, guns, none of that. Me and Cash got years in this game because we use our heads to get this bread, so just follow our lead, yo!" Smack Down intervened.

****

America and Mr. Frosty Blow walked out of Platinum Beats Studio at 12:47 a.m. and talked about the collaboration track they had done. It was a song they called "Likin' Her". On it, America sung the hook and they both rapped a verse.

"This was supposed to be my session, my song an' shit. I don't know how I let you take over my session. We were supposed to be workin' on a song fo' me, not you," Mr. Frosty Blow said with a chuckle, and a childish look on his face, slowly shaking his head.

"All those hits you got under ya belt, boy, shut up," America replied, giving Mr. Frosty Blow a playful nudge on the shoulder.

The *Love & Trap Muzik, Pittsburgh*'s camera crew was still recording while security stood by. Security was always on duty when the show was filming.

Suddenly, a Beleza Mercedes-Benz Sprinter pulled up, and Dominican Flames and her people poured out. Monte Bucks had prearranged for the confrontation to happen. He wanted America and Dominican Flames beef to take place while they were filming. He knew that Dominican Flames would be upset about the leaked footage that America had sold him.

"There they go right there, Smack. All lovie-dovie an' shit," Hitter B. said before Dominican Flames and her goons pulled up and jumped out.

Smack Down had pulled up and parked on the opposite side of the street of Platinum Beats only seconds before.

"We need to go holla at that lame," Hitter B. said, not noticing Dominican Flames stepping to America.

"Nigga, hol' up! You don't see all that shit goin' on, and what the fuck you got ya strap out fo'? Ya dumb ass don't see security and cameras all over the spot. Nigga, I ain't tryna catch no Fed case 'bout no stupid shit!"

"Oh, shit! I ain't even see them muthafuckas jump, bro. My bad," Hitter B. said, getting back into the car, tucking his strap.

"Bitch, how the fuck you playin' me? I do all this shit fo' you and ya moms, and you cross me? Who the fuck gave you my footage?" Dominican Flames yelled, giving America an icy glare, balling her fists up.

"What the fuck?" Mr. Frosty Blow was ready to draw his strap until he realized that he was on camera. Besides that, security had rushed both parties.

"Get the fuck outta here wit' that bullshit! Don't be fuckin' jumpin' out on me like you gon' do some'in' to me!" America yelled back.

"Yo, get the fuck off me. Why the fuck is y'all holdin' me," Mr. Frosty Blow said, tussling with security.

"Nigga, you better calm the fuck down. This shit is between me and this snake-ass bitch! You ain't got nothin' to do wit' this," Dominican Flames told Mr. Frosty Blow.

"Yo, let me the fuck go," Mr. Frosty Blow said, pushing security.

"Look at that lame actin' tough. I can't stand that nigga," Hitter B. said, but he barely knew Mr. Frosty Blow.

"Cah, you don't want this, you really don't. Believe me!" Mr. Frosty Blow said to Dominican Flames, his mind on the strap he was carrying.

"Why don't I, nigga?" Dominican Flames said,

lunging towards the two rappers.

"Uggghhh, bitch!" America swung on Dominican Flames.

"Bitch. Taking my fuckin' footage!" Dominican Flames swung back, but security stood between the two of them. Then, somehow, Dominican Flames got loose. "Aaaaarrrgghh, get the fuck—" Dominican Flames grabbed a hand full of America's hair and they started scuffling. Before Mr. Frosty Blow and Dominican Flames' goons could get into it, security intervened and broke up the fight.

"We out!" Smack Down said, shifting his car into drive. "We could lay on 'em. Get 'em when this shit die down. It'll seem like that bitch Dominican did the shit," Hitter B. said, still trying to put in work.

"I said we out! The police is 'bout to be around this bitch. We Downtown Pittsburgh," Smack Down said, pulling away from the drama.

He had seen all he wanted to see, and he wondered what America would bring to the show. Like everyone else, he had gotten the email about her taking her mother's place on the show, but he knew little about her. All he knew was that she was young, sexy, talented, and as far as he could see, full of drama, and he liked it all.

CHAPTER 13:

WRONG ONE TO FUCK WIT'

Later that night, America and Ren sat at their mother's stunning stone home nestled on a 6.2-acre tabletop lot in Fox Chapel. They were listening to the tracks Boom Bap had emailed America.

"That bitch is trippin'. Don't worry 'bout her, sis. You know how she is; she just be talkin' shit. She ain't really tryna take it there. She doin' all that for the show," Ren said after hearing about America and Dominican Flames' confrontation.

"Oh, I ain't worried 'bout her ass. I'm just mad as hell that I gotta go to this bitch's spot fo' the teaser party tomorrow."

"Don't go!"

"I can't not go, shit's mandatory. We're filming for the show the entire night. Plus, the DJ is gon' play me and Mr. Frosty Blow's new single, so I gots to be there. I'm just mad that it's gon' be at her club."

"That shit hard right there," Ren said, bobbing his head to a Drake-styled beat.

"You like that?" America asked, bobbing her head and motioning her hands in the air. She mentally fit her lyrics to the track, then she started flowing to the beat under her breath.

"Hey, sis, you talk to Ma today?" Ren asked, turning the beat down.

"Earlier. She had therapy today. I was goin' to go over there, but I had the show to do. You talk to her?"

"Nah. I was goin' to go over there, too, but I hate seeing her like that, you know?"

"Yea. Did you catch that shit on the news about that nigga who shot her?"

"Nah. When you hit me and told me to check that shit out, it was off. I wanted to see who that nigga was, too."

"Why you ain't pull it up online?"

"Oh, you can do that shit? You know I don't know nothin' 'bout that computer shit."

"Hell yea. I got you, tho'," America said as she went to the news' website, and pulled up the news clip about their mother.

"CHANNEL 0 NEWS: STANDOFF ENDS IN MAN'S ARREST", the headline read at the bottom of the screen as the news reporter talked in detail about the ordeal.

"A suspect in the reality star shooting was held up in an apartment for three hours before surrendering.

"A little before 4:00 P.M., SWAT officers entered the house on 28th Street, and arrested the only occupant, Andrew Kaus, twenty-six, from Homewood, more than three hours after the standoff began. The incident started about 1:00 P.M., after police received an anonymous call about the shooting suspect's whereabouts, authorities said. When Pittsburgh Police arrived, the suspect threatened them, and that's when Kaus displayed his gun through the downstairs window.

"Police then spent more than three hours trying to get Kaus to come out, hailing him with a loudspeaker, urging him to come out of the house. When he did not cooperate, SWAT officers threw canisters of tear gas into the house, and drove the suspect to surrender. That's the latest. Reporting live from Lawrenceville, Guy Speaks, Channel 0 News."

"You know I gotta handle this, don't you, sis?"

"Hell yea. We can't let him get away wit' what he did to Ma."

"Say no mo'," Ren said, thumbing a number into his cell phone. "I'm all over this shit," he said, placing his phone to his ear as his cell phone rang.

****

AT THE HOME OF C.O. GENE HOOKER

"See, now there's a huge misconception about black guys and big dicks. I have strip-searched a thousand of these fucks, and only seven out of ten of 'em got big dicks. I gotta bigger dick than some of these muthafuckas."

"Some of these black guys I've given an apology to 'cause their dicks are an embarrassment to the black race," C.O. Hooker said with a chuckle. He was entertaining his wife during dinner at their Sewickley home.

"Oh, Gene, you're so silly."

"Oh, hol' up, babe. I gotta take this call," C.O.

Hooker said, stepping away from the dinner table. "Sup, Ren? No, I haven't seen it. Online? Okay, I'll give it a view. Ha,

that's what I'm talkin' 'bout. I'll check everything out and get back to you."

"Okay, I'm back, babe."

"Gene, I don't wanna hear no more about black guys' dicks," C.O. Hooker's wife said, chuckling. She was enjoying his company. He had an hour before he had to go in to work. He worked third shift at the Allegheny County Jail. Every night after putting their kids to bed, she sat with him as he ate dinner. His shift made him sleep all day, so they spent an hour or two together before he went to work.

C.O. Hooker kissed his wife, and smiled as she laughed at him.

"All right, babe, I won't say any more about them little black dicks," he said, making her laugh some more. He continued to joke, but the call he had received from Ren was no laughing matter. Ren had told him to track down his mother's shooter at the county jail and take care of him, and that's what he planned to do. So, before he went to work, he pulled up the news footage on his laptop, and made a mental note of the suspect's name and arrest date.

Gene and Ren had grown up together, played football together, and had even joined the army together. After the service, it was hard for them to find work, so Ren went back to the streets, and Gene settled for a job at the Allegheny County Jail, and with the help of Ren, he flooded the jail with cell phones and drugs. One forty-dollar cell phone sold for twenty-five hundred in some jails, and they made ten times as much from drugs.

Ren had helped him do more than just survive paycheck to paycheck; he allowed him to buy his home, pay for a big wedding, and save money for his kids' college funds. Now Ren was calling for a favor, and Gene liked doing favors for Ren because they paid well.

After seeing the news footage and hearing about Dominican Flames stepping to his sister, Ren felt that he had to settle the score by taking action. He wasn't going to let anybody get away with threatening his sister, and he definitely wasn't going to let Andrew Kaus get away with shooting his mother.

Dressed in all-black, he drove to Reflections nightclub during closing. He wanted to go into the club and shoot it up, but when he pulled up, there were police and security everywhere. After the shooting, Dominican Flames had stepped up her security. Ren even saw the *Love & Trap Muzik, Pittsburgh* camera crew lurking around. Seeing this made him rethink his plans. He couldn't risk going to jail while his mother was still in the hospital, and his sister's life was being threatened.

Driving back home, Ren thought about the relationship he and Dominican Flames once had, and he thought about how recklessly he was thinking. From time to time, he had to remember that he was no longer in the military, but at the same time, he couldn't let anybody disrespect his family. Even if he didn't do anything to Dominican Flames, he knew he had to send her a message to let her know that she could be touched. It wouldn't be easy, and harming her could definitely cause a family feud that could lead to bodies lying dead in the streets, so he knew that he had to play it smart.

Taking his cell phone out of the cupholder of his mother's repaired Vanquish, he thumbed America's number into it, and pressed send to call her. After a few rings, she answered, half-asleep, "Sup, brother?"

"Text me that security guard's number; I need to get at him," Ren told his sister.

"What security guard?" America asked.

"The one who sold you that footage."

"Oh, okay, I got you. Brother, what are you up to?"

"Just text me his number."

"Okay, just be careful, bro, please," America told her only sibling.

"I got this, sis. Don't worry," Ren replied before hanging up with his sister. A few minutes later, the security guard's number popped up in Ren's message box: *Pedro- 412-777-8888.*

Fifteen minutes later, Ren met with Pedro. In exchange for five thousand dollars, Pedro provided Ren with Dominican Flames' address.

"Now step back!" Ren told Pedro, walking up to the Mercedes-Benz Sprinter Pedro was driving with an AR-15 in his hand.

"Don't, amigo!" Pedro said, trying to stop Ren from

shooting up the Sprinter.

"Look, fam, this bitch can get shot up by itself, or you can get shot up wit' it," Ren said, giving Pedro a menacing look, letting him know he meant business. Without any more hesitation, Pedro stepped to the side, and watched Ren lift his assault rifle toward the Sprinter.

Ren shot holes into the Sprinter customized by Lexani Motocars. He shot out its windows, body, tires, and destroyed the forty-eight-inch curved 4k VHD TV and other electronics inside of it.

****

C.O. Hooker popped cell one on Unit 6D at 3:18 a.m., at the Allegheny County Jail. Hearing his cell door being popped, Andrew Kaus opened his eyes.

"Man, what is goin' on?" Andrew said, feeling irritated. "I'm not answerin' no mo' questions. I tol' you muthafuckas everything," he continued to say, thinking federal agents wanted to question him, but before he could sit up and gather himself, C.O. Hooker was standing over him.

"Stand up, and turn around!" C.O. Hooker told him firmly.

"Maaaan, what the—"

"STAND UP, AND TURN AROUND, NOW!"

"This is crazy," Andrew said, turning around. Before he could say another word, C.O. Hooker had put him in a chokehold.

"He-help," Andrew gasped as he struggled for his life. "Ssshhh. Shut the fuck up," C.O. Hooker whispered in his ear as he tightened his grip around Andrew's neck. "Just go to sleep, muthafucka. Eternity's waiting fo' you in hell," C.O. Hooker continued saying in a deadly murmur as he choked the life out of Andrew. After a few minutes, Andrew stopped struggling. Slowly squatting down with Andrew still coiled in his arms, C.O. Hooker used his 6'5", 298-pound body to end Andrew's life. He placed one hand on the back of Andrew's head, and his other hand at the base of his chin and snapped his neck. Then he dragged his body and leaned it against his bunk.

Removing the sheet from his bed, C.O. Hooker tore two long strips from it, and tied it into a noose. After tying it to a metal vent in the cell, he hoisted Andrew's neck into its loop, and let his body drop.

"Eww, shit, ya ass stink," C.O. Hooker said, offended by the stench that had started filling the cell. Andrew had pissed and shit himself.

Standing back, C.O. Hooker thoroughly looked over the crime scene, and then called for medical assistance. "We need a medic in 6D. It looks to be an apparent suicide attempt. Please hurry. We need a medic to 6D!"

CHAPTER 14:

YOU WIN SOME/YOU LOSE SOME

While at Buck's Enterprises, the cast of LTMP sat at the boardroom table. DQ Dawg, Smack Down, Boom Bap and America were on one side of the table, and Dominican Flames, Mr. Frosty Blow, Blocks N Bricks and Making Hitz were on the other. Monte Bucks sat at the head of one side of the table, and the opposite side was prepared for Money King, but she had other obligations to attend to.

Monte Bucks had gotten word about America and Dominican Flames' beef. He had also heard about Dominican Flames' Sprinter van being shot up, and he wanted to address the matter, as well as safeguard himself from any legal ramification. So, he had his lawyers draw up a disclaimer that stated that the company would not be held liable for any illegal actions of its cast members, and he wanted all of them to sign it, or leave the show. He also wanted to brief them about the upcoming teaser party, and inform them that Hip Hop Weekly was flying in to interview them individually. They were doing a LTMP edition of their magazine.

"Today, I'm flying in Hip Hop Weekly. Matter of fact, they should have landed already. Anyway, everybody will have a chance to give an interview.

"As far as upcoming events, DQ Dawg is doing a video shoot today. It's going to start in a couple hours, and end at Reflections. Tomorrow, we got the teaser party, and also, today is Money King's birthday, so this whole weekend gon' be lit. We gon' do it big at Reflections, red carpet and all," Monte said, addressing the cast members.

"Why everything gotta be at Reflections?" America muttered, sucking her teeth.

"Fuck you, bitch! You ain't gotta come!" Dominican Flames shot back.

"Whoa! Whoa! Hol' up! It's gon' be at Reflections because I'm keeping everything in-house. Why would I give another club the exposure?" Monte Bucks said.

"That bitch shot my fuckin' Sprinter up! She lucky she still breathin'!" Dominican Flames stood up, and said.

"What, bitch? I don't know what the fuck you talkin' 'bout; I ain't shoot up shit!" America stood up and said.

"Yea, okay! Just like you don't know about my footage, lying-ass bitch! You know exactly what the fuck I'm talkin' 'bout," Dominican Flames said. Her blood was boiling.

"SIT DOWN! Sit y'all asses down!" Monte demanded, and America and Dominican Flames sat down.

The boardroom was the one place security was not needed when it came to the cast members, even though they stood close by, outside the boardroom. Hearing all the commotion, they rushed in, but Monte waved them off. He didn't need security to control his cast members. All he needed to do was raise his voice, and show that he meant business.

"Like I was saying, DQ Dawg is doin' his video Saturday, and I would like to congratulate him and Making Hitz fo' their hit single 'She Like It From The Baaack, hittin' number four on the Billboard charts, and number one on USA Today's Urban Airplay charts," Monte announced. Boom Bap and Making Hitz's eyes connected and locked.

"And DQ Dawg is featured in the Song Of The Week section of USA Today."

The room congratulated DQ Dawg with applause. "And, I don't know if any of y'all have been paying any attention, but I wanna proudly say that the LTMP webpage has close to forty million views. They lookin' fo' us, people. They really wanna see us win wit' this new show, so everybody keep up the good work. We'll meet up next week, regular day and time."

Everyone clapped and stood up to leave. "Oh, and one mo' thing. Make sure y'all give our executive producer, Money King, a birthday shout out," Monte said, concluding the board meeting. Everyone exited the boardroom, having small conversations with each other.

"Monte, let me holla at you fo' a sec'," Mr. Frosty Blow said, approaching Monte. He wanted to talk to him about the details of his sister's birthday dinner.

During the meeting, America had caught Smack Down staring at her several times. Leaving the meeting, he stopped her in her tracks. "What was you doin' wit' that sucka-ass nigga, Frosty, the other night?" he asked her.

"He ain't no sucka, and we did a song, Smack Down!" America replied, twisting her lips and bobbing her head with a coy smile on her face

"You comin to Money's birthday dinner?" Smack Down asked.

"Yea, I'll be at ya baby mama's birthday dinner."

"Oh, you know about that? You know that's my people, huh?"

“Who doesn't? Besides, that’s my mom's girl.”

"Yea, that is right. We all went to Langley together; I don't know why I ain't put that together."

"Stop playin', you knew that. Ya ass is just up to no good. Bye, Smack Down."

"Hol' up, I wanna do a song wit' you," Smack Down said, stopping America from walking away. "Take my number," he continued.

“A’ight, what is it?" America asked, pulling out her phone. Smack Down took it and put his number in it. "Hit me. Let's set some'in' up fo' the show," he said, handing America her phone back.

"Smack! Yo! Let me holla at'cha, dukes." Making Hitz interrupted America and Smack Down's exchange of words.

"Hey, I'll holla at you later. I'm on my way to see my moms," America said before walking off.

"Cool. Hit me later, tho’," Smack Down said.

“A’ight," America said, walking towards the elevator.

"Holla at me!" Smack Down shouted as the elevator doors shut on America.

"I said a'ight!" America yelled back with a chuckle

before the elevator doors fully closed.

On the inside of the elevator, America watched as the numbers counted down to the garage level. The elevator sounded as its doors slid open. The sound of America's spiked, suede Giuseppe wedge sandals bouncing off the concrete echoed throughout the garage. Reaching into her YSL Cassandre leather clutch for her keys, she was caught by surprise by two men running up on her. Her life flashed before her eyes.

"OH GOD! Aaagghh, oh my God, oh my God," America yelped. The shots from the two paintball guns the shooters yielded, covered her Maje-printed, silk jersey, and made her drop her Saint Laurent clutch. Her iPhone, covered in its Moschino hard case, dropped and bounced off the ground, then a lyrical copper Rolls-Royce Wraith pulled up slowly and Dominican Flames stepped out of it. "Next time it won't be paint; you'll be covered in blood, bitch!" she said to America, and got back into her Wraith with her two henchmen and pulled off.

"BITCH! YOU BITCH! IT'S ON!" America screamed, watching them pull off.

A stranger walked up to America and asked, "Hey, miss, you okay? I saw the whole thing. I was watchin' from my car," he said.

"Yea, I'll be okay. Thanks," America replied, picking up her clutch and phone.

"You sure?" the stranger asked.

As America began to talk, the stranger struck her twice with the butt of his gun, knocking her out.

****

Later that day, at Money King's birthday dinner, a small group of family and friends gathered at a private location to celebrate Money's born day, including Monte Bucks. Most of the LTMP had just sent gifts and well wishes.

Money wasn't too fond of being around strangers. Plus, she was over protective of her son, and didn't allow strangers to even see what he looked like. After being shot, she was extra careful about who she associated with.

Mr. Frosty Blow tapped his fork against his Ace of Spade's bottle to get everyone's attention, then cleared his throat for the second time. "Sis, on behalf of everyone here..." Mr. Frosty Blow paused, and looked at Smack Down, who sat beside his sister, Money, and their son.

“We wanna thank you. If it wasn't fo' ya vision, and Monte's bucks..." Everyone laughed.

“No, seriously, if it wasn't fo' y'all, we wouldn't be here. Close to forty million views without an episode ever shown is big. I just wanna thank you, sis."

Everyone applauded as Smack Down's cell phone vibrated. It was the third time since Mr. Frosty had started his speech. Hitter B. had tried to call him the first two times, but this time, it was JB. Sensing something was wrong, he took the call.

As everyone saluted Money by raising their glasses or tapping their silverware against their champagne flutes, Smack Down tilted over to Money and told her, "I need to take this call, looks important."

"Okay." Money understood.

"And I know shit's gon' get bigger and bigger," Mr. Frosty Blow said, taking his seat. "Yo! Where the fuck you goin'?" he asked Smack Down, feeling disrespected by him leaving the table while he was still speaking.

"Bro, don't do that, please. Not here, not now," Money said to her brother as Smack Down walked away as if he hadn't heard a word Frosty Blow was saying.

Everybody at the table knew about their history, but knew that they both had enough respect for Money not to beef around her.

"Yo! What's so fuckin' important that you muthafuckas keep callin' me? Y'all know I'm at dinner wit' Money and my son!" Smack Down said through clenched teeth, holding the phone with a death grip to his mouth. The disturbance had him hot. "WHAT? You bullshittin'. Where he got her? Get the fuck outta here, this dumb muthafucka! You there wit' him now? Be right there!"

Now Smack Down understood why JB had been calling so urgently. Hitter B. had kidnapped America, and he was ready to beat her to a bloody pulp for information about her money's whereabouts. Not only was Hitter B. threatening to take away his son's uncle, but now he was doing shit that could get them all locked up for life. Smack Down knew how to keep the streets separate from his family, but this move that Hitter B. had made was bringing the streets to his family.

"Money, I gotta go. Some'in' crazy just happened," Smack Down whispered in Money's ear.

"Some street shit?" Money asked, looking at Smack Down with her nostrils flared, and an angry look on her face.

"Yea, sort of," Smack Down answered.

"See, that's why we ain't together no more. You just can't leave the streets alone."

"We'll talk tonight."

"We don't need to talk, and ya ass might not see me tonight."

"What?"

"Just go!"

"Dad gotta step out. I'll see you later, kiddo. Love you," Smack Down said to his son, rubbing the top of his head, then kissing him on the forehead.

"Hey, can I get everybody's attention fo' a minute? I wanna thank everybody fo' comin' out to celebrate Money's birthday, but sorry, I gotta slip away on some business," Smack Down told the dinner guests.

Money rolled her eyes and smacked her teeth.

"What the fuck you mean you gotta go on some business shit? We all got business to handle. You think Mr. Bucks doesn't have business to handle, or my sister ain't got business to handle? You need to learn how to sacrifice. Family comes first, yo!" Mr. Frosty Blow said, standing up at the table. "See, I let you slide when you disrespected me, but now you disrespectin' my sis," he continued to express.

"Man, I gotta go! I ain't tryna hear that shit you

talkin' 'bout," Smack Down said, walking away from the dinner table.

"What the fuck you say, nigga?" Mr. Frosty Blow stood up, and asked. He wanted to go after him, but Money put her hand up, and nudged her head towards their son. He was listening to everything that was being said. "Bro, let him go, please," she said, calming her brother down.

****

It took Smack Down roughly twenty minutes to get to Bass-Filled Studio. "He got her upstairs in Recording Room One. He's seconds from beatin' the shit outta ol' gal. The fool got plastic laid down an' everything," JB told Smack Down after letting him into the studio.

"What the fuck, man! Why the fuck you ain't stop him?" Smack Down asked JB with a disappointed look on his face.

"I did! He busted her head before I got here. She did tell him that she got a mill-ticket stashed somewhere, tho', but he said he wasn't gon' do shit else till you got here. Oh, and, he said Flames and her goons hit her up wit' paint guns before he grabbed her up, so most of the red shit on her is paint," JB said.

"What kinda shit is that?" Smack Down asked.

"He said Flames told America next time it was gon' be blood an' shit," JB told Smack Down with a chuckle.

"Now that bitch a killa? This reality TV shit got muthafuckas goin' crazy," Smack Down said as they entered Recording Room One.

Hitter B. was a mild mannered young boy from the hood, but shortly after being hired to produce and engineer for Smack Down and the Smack Dizzy Boyz, he started using Percocets and Molly, and started doing things he thought would make him fit in.

Smack Down normally ignored his hard-acting routine, but now Hitter B. had taken things to another level—kidnapping and torture. He had taken America to their newly renovated studio where her cries would go unheard.

Smack Down had given him a hundred thousand dollars to upgrade his studio. Instead, Hitter B. had bought an old car lot, and turned the duplex into a state-of-the-art studio complex with all up-to-date equipment, and renovated it. The upper level was completely sound-proofed and remodeled.

"Aaaah! Help!" America screamed.

"Scream all you want, bitch! Can't nobody hear ya dumb ass! This muthafucka's soundproof, so scream all you want!"

"HELLLLP!"

JB and Smack Down could hear America scream when they opened the door to Studio Room One, but hadn't heard anything before that. Her screams were absorbed by the cellulose-fiber panels and special acoustical polyurethane foam tiles that covered the walls once the door was shut again.

“Smack! Smack! Why are you doing this? I told you I’ll give you the money. Don’t kill me, please!” America pleaded.

Hitter B. continued to hit America in the head with his pistol. "Shut up, hoe!" he ordered when he saw Smack Down. "Bitch gotta mill-ticket stashed, bro!" he told him with a devilish grin on his face. Smack Down could tell that he was high on something.

“Sma-Smack Down, please. Why you got him doin' this to me?" America asked.

"Let me holla at you, fam," Smack Down said to Hitter B., pulling him to the side.

"Smack, please!" America continued to beg and plead for her life.

"I told ya ass to shut the fuck up, bitch!" Hitter B. said, pointing his strap at America.

JB shook his head, watching Hitter B.

"What, nigga? You gotta problem?” Hitter B. asked JB.

"Let me holla at you, yo!" Smack Down said again in a firm voice, waving Hitter B. over to a corner.

"What up, big bro? We on, my nigga. All we gotta do is make a call and collect the paper," Hitter B. said as he walked over to Smack Down.

"Yea, that's what's up. Let me ask you a question, tho’: did you tell anybody 'bout this? You know, this idea of yours," Smack Down asked.

"Nah, bruh. I was gon' let you know, but I knew you was gon' be busy today. I knew y'all had that meeting today, so shit was perfect fo' me to grab that bitch, you know?"

"I feel you. You got plastic down, an' the whole shit, huh?"
"Well, you know, bro, I ain't tryna leave her blood in ya spot."

"Right? So, get the number off of her so we can collect," Smack Down muttered.

"You know we gotta kill the bitch after we collect, right?" "Kill her?"

"Yea, hell yea. She knows who did this to her. We can't take no chances. The good thing about it is, everybody'll think that bitch Dominican Flames did the shit, you know?" Hitter B. said, thinking he had everything worked out.

"Yea, you right. We can't let her testify on us. I'm just thinking, tho', what about that big teaser party we're havin' tomorrow. They gon' be lookin' fo' her to show up."

"Long as we get rid of the body, we'll be a'ight."

"So, we gon' have to off whoever brings the money, too?" "Yea, if that's what we gotta do."

"Yo, you thought of everything, bro. That's what's up," Smack Down said, slapping Hitter B. five, and pulling him in close.

"We came up wit' this one, big bro," Hitter B. said, hugging Smack Down tightly. He released him, and smiled, then he turned towards America to gather more information. "Bitch, what's ya—" Smack Down blew a hole in the back of Hitter B.'s head, walked up on his body after he fell, and shot him in the head again to make sure he was dead.

"Agh! No!" America screamed.

"Stupid muthafucka," Smack Down said, tucking his strap into his waist. "Untie her," he told JB.

America sobbed. Her heart was beating at a fast, frantic, rapid pace as she stared at Hitter B.'s lifeless body on the studio floor. She hadn't even heard Smack Down tell JB to untie her, so when JB started walking towards her, she started screaming again.

"You gon' be a'ight," JB told America as he untied her. "'Bout time you killed that reckless nigga. What we gon' do wit' her?"

"I'm takin' her home," Smack Down said.

"Fo' real? Aw, thank you, Smack Down!" America said, running up to Smack Down with her arms open.

WE TRAP OR DIE 135

"And him?" JB asked, looking over the remains of Hitter B.'s skull.

"Let one of the lil homies find him. They got keys; they'll find his ass. Get rid of the plastic, rope, chair and ya clothes, tho'," Smack down told JB.

"What about his car?"

"Leave it."

CHAPTER 15:

I'M MY SISTA'S KEEPER

In the wee hours of the morning, Smack Down drove America to her mother's Fox Chapel estate.

"Thank you, Smack," America said, holding a rag to her head after examining herself in the mirror. She was happy that Hitter B. hadn't damaged her face too much.

At first, America was skeptical about Smack Down knowing where she lived, but the more she thought about him putting two bullets into her kidnapper, the more she trusted him. Besides that, she had called her brother and told him what had happened, so he knew that she was coming with company. She knew that would raise a red flag with her brother, and he would be on point when they arrived.

"Look, America, I'm truly sorry about what happened," Smack Down murmured, shaking his head. "I didn't know anything about that nigga's plans of kidnappin' you," he told her.

"Shit, I'm just glad you were there to save me. He was goin' to kill me, wasn't he?"

Smack Down briefly closed his eyes, and shook the thought of Hitter B. killing America out of his head. "Yea, that was his plan," he said, confirming Hitter B.'s murderous plot to kill America.

"I owe you my life, Smack," America said, releasing a thankful sigh.

"Nah, you don't owe me shit. Matter of fact, send me ya medical bill. I got that."

"You want me to bill you six dollars?"

"Hm, what you mean six dollars?" Smack Down asked, looking over at America nursing her wounds.

"Yea, six dollars. I'm not goin' to the hospital, I'm just gon' pop a few Advil and call it a night. I just want to take a hot bath and crawl into my bed, you hear me? Turn up here," America said as she continued to direct Smack Down to her mother's estate.

"Maaan, you crazy. You're goin' to the hospital, even if I gotta take you. You might have a concussion or some'in'," Smack Down cautioned her.

"I'm good. They would ask too many questions, and what am I goin' to tell them? I got beat by a crazed kidnapper named Hitter B.? I can't do that, now can I? And if I did that, they'll link the dead body laying in ya studio to me," America improvised.

"Damn, I ain't think about that," Smack Down said, scratching his head, mentally checking for any other loose ends he may have left untied.

"I'll be a'ight. I'ma big girl. A couple ice packs, a few Advil, my bed, and I'll be a'ight. But, like I said, I owe you," America said again, looking over at Smack Down with a half-smile on her face. "If you need anything, let me know," she continued as Smack Down smiled back at her.

“A'ight, maybe there is some'in' you can do fo' me," Smack Down said as he paused and stroked his goatee with his hand. "Invest some of that guap into my next move. I'm tryna make a couple mo' moves and get out the game. If you invest, we can make that happen."

"Oh, you tryna cop big, and quit the game, huh? Make this left," America asked as she continued to direct Smack Down to her estate.

"What you know 'bout coppin?"

"My grandma and Ma taught me everything there is to know 'bout the streets. My grandma was one of the biggest drug dealers in our hood in the late eighties and nineties. That's how we know that bitch Dominican. My grandma did a lil bit of time fo' coppin' from her father, Brooklyn Pete. When she got outta jail, she fell back, and got into real estate. She the one who got this spot fo' my moms, and a few other spots fo' people on the show. So, you know, I know about the game," America explained. "Go up this driveway," she continued.

"Daaammmn, this ya spot?" Smack Down looked over the estate in awe. "This is insane," he said. The estate was up there with him and Money's estate.

"Thank you," America said as she gathered her belongings to exit the car.

"So, are you gon' make this power move wit' me?" Smack Down asked as he pulled into the driveway of the 6.2-acre estate.

"What you need? Just let me know. I got you."

"Five hundred racks. I'm tryna go hard."

"I got you."

"Yo, A, what the fuck happened?" America's brother asked, running up to Smack Down's Phantom, trying to pry the door open to get to his sister. Smack Down unlocked the door for him. "I'ma fuckin' kill some-fucking-body. Who the fuck did this?" Ren ranted, walking back and forth.

"Bro, calm down. I took care of it," America told her brother as she stepped out of Smack Down's luxury car. "Bro, I'm cool," she told her brother, backing him away from her. "Smack, holla at me in the mornin', early. You know we gotta big day tomorrow," she said to Smack Down.

"Damn, we do got that damn party tomorrow. I almost forgot. We can wait if you want to."

"Nah, we ain't gotta wait. We just gotta move early."

"Bet. What's early fo' you?"

"'Bout six. If not then, we gon' have to wait fo' a couple days ’cause we got the party tomorrow night, and the next day, I gotta pick my moms up from the hospital, and you know that's gon' be an all-day thing."

"Oh, ya moms is comin' home? That's what's up. I'll be here tomorrow at six then."

"A, come on! Hooker's on his way over here. We gon' do some'in' 'bout this shit," Ren said, getting impatient.

"Cool, I'll see you then," America said to Smack Down, ignoring her brother's rants. She blew Smack Down a kiss.

"Don't play," Smack Down said to her, smiling before he pulled off.

After America had told Ren and C.O. Hooker what happened, he called Dominican Flames. He couldn't get revenge on the dead man laying in Smack Down's studio, but he definitely planned on settling the score with Dominican Flames and her street goons for threatening his sister's life. He wanted to kill them, but America had begged him not to bring any more heat to their family. She explained how it would be bad for them, and would possibly lead to an investigation that neither of their families needed.

"Listen, either you and the two sucka-ass niggas who hit my sista up wit' them paint guns meet me, or shit gon' really go down. You know me, and you know I don't give a fuck about no reality TV show or none of that shit! Y'all muthafuckas ain't gon' keep disrespectin' my family. Oh, yea? Well, meet me. I just wanna holla at them niggas. We ain't gotta use the guns; I'll see them niggas wit' my hands. Yea, you got my word, this time. Wherever. Langley High School parking lot is cool; I'll be there in a half hour," Ren said to Dominican Flames.

She had agreed to hash things out with a street brawl between her goons and Ren.

The clock on Ren's cell phone was approaching 1:00 a.m., and the night was still young for those who played the streets. He mentally prepared himself for hand-to-hand combat as his tires hissed, rolling over the terrain of Langley High School's parking lot. Headlights shined and lit up the faces of Ren and his two passengers as they pulled into the lot, parked, and got out of the car.

"Shit, you might need my help, bro."

"Mine too. Them some big muthafuckas," C.O. Hooker said, and America agreed with a chuckle.

"I got this," Ren said, stepping out of the car, into the ring of headlights.

The fist of Dominican Flames' humungous enforcer slamming into his hand sounded like a baseball slamming into a mitt. He stood opposite of Ren. His muscles bulged as he stood in his wife beater, ready to bring the pain.

Ren removed his hoodie, but left his wife beater on. His muscular body was heavily tattooed with Asian and Japanese artwork; skulls, dragons, tigers and Samurai masks. He stood 5'11, 250 pounds of well sculpted flesh tailor fitted to every muscle in his body. He cracked his knuckles and neck as he sized his opponents up.

His opponents were also muscle heads, standing imminently around their lady boss, Dominican Flames. The four giants stood over her like mountains. They oozed toughness, and all were known to live in the violent world as bodyguards, hard asses and street thugs with a reputation to murder.

Dominican Flames' doormen and bodyguards knew nothing of Ren, as he knew nothing of them, so they knew nothing of each other's training or fighting experiences. On the other hand, Dominican Flames knew almost everything about Ren. They had grown up together, and had an interest in one another up until his grandmother was indicted for her father's mistakes. Ren blamed her father for his grandmother's arrest and indictment, and since then, there had always been some animosity between them, a smoldering enmity their grandmother and mother overlooked. They understood the actions and consequences of the game. Their grandmother's success was owed to Dominican Flames' parents. What America and Ren didn't know was their grandmother was gratefully rewarded for her loyalty, but at this point, none of that mattered.

Ren was ready to punish, even kill those who had threatened his sister.

Before they arrived, Dominican Flames started to tell her men-for-hire about Ren's four-year military background and about his one-punch knock out skills. She also knew that he had taken up martial arts when they were kids, but she didn't think it would matter. Her men were also skillful fighters. Men on both sides knew that one wrong move, no matter how skillful you were, could send the most trained

fighter into a panic, making him forget all about what they were taught to do.

During his military years, Ren had traveled and learned about different cultures and styles of hand combat, including Judo and kickboxing. He veered these fighting skills towards more practical, full-contact, street style martial arts. His teacher had once graced the cover of *Black Belt* magazine. Now his skills stood to be challenged by hired, fully trained, licensed security guards.

When the security guard smashing his fist into his

hand saw Ren take off his hoodie, he studied his body's muscular frame and was not impressed. "I'ma tear ya ass apart, boy!" he said to Ren in Spanish.

"I don't know what the fuck he said, but it sounded scary," C.O. Hooker joked, not afraid at all. He had also gone to the military with Ren, and knew a few fighting techniques himself. He was also deadly with his hands, and had the muscle and weight to back them. If he wanted, he could crush another man with his bare hands. He had killed shortly before this grudge match, and would not hesitate to do it again.

America and Dominican Flames gazed at each other. Their nostrils flared, and they only broke eye contact when the bodyguard and Ren squared up to fight. There would be no mercy given, and neither of them were seeking forgiveness. Moving in a 180-degree circle, the bodyguard moved light on his feet, as did Ren. Ren took notice of his possible training in martial arts.

Standing off froth the bodyguard, Ren's eyes roamed around, locked into his opponent's movements. He wanted him to move in, but wouldn't allow him to move in too close. He knew that could be fatal. Yet, he needed him to come in close enough for his short reach.

After a few seconds, Ren realized that the bodyguard was waiting on the same thing, so Ren gave him what he was waiting for. Moving in on the guard, Ren's shorter body bobbed with buoyancy, similar to that of Mike Tyson. He bobbed and weaved, and threw a machine gun-like volley of punches. One caught the bodyguard once on the left side of his face, leaving his ear ringing. Seeing Ren retreating made the bodyguard move in. He went at Ren like a bear, arms and claws extended for the kill. Ren waited for the guard to get within arms-length, and stepped to the side, sending the guard flying past him. The scene was that of a bull charging a matador.

As the bodyguard flew past him, Ren threw a right-hand punch that struck the guard in the left temple. The impact of the blow sent the large man plummeting perpendicular to the ground, face first. He was unconscious before he hit the hard concrete. The hit of force split the guard's head wide open. Flesh and blood smeared the harsh texture of the gravel, tearing his skin into shreds of brown skin and white flesh as blood trailed.

Ren looked back over his shoulder at the large structure of man who had collapsed like a falling skyscraper, then he pointed to another bodyguard, "You! Come on, let's go!"

The bodyguard who had gotten knocked out began to wake up, feeling groggy, but Ren walked over to him and gave him a swift kick to his bloody face. "UGH!" He knocked him back out, in need of time to deal with his friend.

Going around in circles, the two street gladiators felt each other out. The second bodyguard had a chance to see Ren's skills, and he knew to be careful. Out of the two bodyguards, the second was the better fighter. Taking a sideways stance, he danced and bobbed back and forth, knees half-bent. He sent two kicks Ren's way; one aimed at his head, the other at his chest, but neither connected.

"Nice!" Ren said.

The second bodyguard threw three more kicks in a

combo, and Ren blocked the force of his kicks with his forearm. The second bodyguard put out his sixth kick, and Ren caught it. Holding on to it tightly, he forced the second bodyguard backwards.

"Oh! Oh!" the bodyguard wailed, feeling himself falling to the ground.

"What the fuck!" Dominican Flames was getting frustrated. Folding her arms across her huge breasts, she shifted her head side to side, and rolled her eyes. "Get the fuck up!" she yelled at the bodyguard.

As Ren approached him, the bodyguard braced himself, applied pressure to his upper back, kicked out his legs, and half-flipped back onto his feet, but only because Ren had allowed him to; he was looking for a good fight.

While they continued to fight, a third bodyguard grabbed the first bodyguard under his arms and dragged the dead sack of flimsy bones and muscles off to the side.

Dominican Flames shook her head. "This is pathetic! Look at these muthafuckas!" she said, disappointed in her security.

Hooker watched the third bodyguard to make sure he wasn't trying to do anything to help his friends, but deep inside, he wished he would, so he could join in on the action. He was proud of how Ren was handling himself, but he was tired of just watching. It was getting boring.

Seeing the third guard moving in his peripheral, Ren lost focus for a minute, leaving enough time for the second guard to swing a punch. Ren saw it too late, and was struck in the face, and his nose immediately began to bleed.

Hooker started walking towards the third bodyguard with anger on his face, and balled fists. "You muthafucka!"

"Yo! Back the fuck off, Hooker! I got this," Ren told his man, wiping blood from his face with the back of his hand.

"Maaan, whatever." Hooker let out a frustrated sigh as he backed up.

America watched, still feeling the pain from the whooping she had taken earlier. She just wanted to go home and sleep. She had seen and been through enough for one day.

Dominican Flames looked over at America, examining her swollen face, and black eye. She tried to figure out where the fresh injuries had come from. She knew that her men hadn't caused them.

Oh my God, this bitch beat herself up for attention. Now Ren thinks we did that shit. Stinkin'-ass bitch! she thought.

"I'ma end this right now," the second guard sneered in Spanish.

"Yea, please end this shit!" Dominican Flames said.

"What the fuck did he say?" Hooker asked America.

"I think something about ending it," America answered. She didn't speak fluent Spanish, but she knew some words from hanging with her ex-friend and manager,

Dominican Flames. Her grandmother and mother spoke Spanish fluently, but America and Ren never cared for the language enough to learn it.

A small amount of time had elapsed, but Ren felt he had been there too long. He also wanted to end the hand-to-hand combat, but he refused to submit or rush himself into a mistake.

Ren threw his own series of kicks, but what happened next caught the guard by surprise. Ren dropped low, and took the second guard off his feet with a leg sweep.

"Oof!" The guard landed on his back, and as he tried to recover, Ren kicked him in the face multiple times.

"Ugh, ugh, ugh!" The guard endured the blows as he covered himself, then he grabbed Ren by the foot and twisted it, sending Ren to the ground off balance.

Gathering themselves, both men were back on their feet, bobbing back and forth again, searching for each other's weakness. Then Ren stopped dancing, and so did the guard. He felt that Ren had had enough, and walked up to him.

Ren headbutted him, and followed that with a punch to the throat, crushing the guard's voice box in his twenty-two-inch neck. The guard gasped, then Ren drove two stiff fingers in a scissor formation into each of his eyes. "You muthafucka!" Ren sputtered.

"Oooh, fuck!" the guard bellowed. Stepping away from Ren, he tried to shake the stars from his eyes, plus escape any further punishment.

Ren Bruce Lee-stepped into the guard's imaginary refuge, and kicked hard as he could, snapping the guard's kneecap inward.

"Oooh, shit!" the guard wailed as he collapsed.

Breathing heavily, Ren walked over to Dominican Flames. Her bodyguards stood between them to protect her. Even the one who had gotten beaten up first. She moved them to the side, and walked up to Ren. He didn't scare her. He had actually turned her on.

"The next time you come for us, you better kill us, or you won't live to see another day. None of y'all!" Ren said.

Dominican Flames pecked Ren on the lips, and Ren wiped her kiss away.

"You got my pussy so wet. You should come home wit' me. I know how to turn a fighter into a lover, baby. You know you miss me," Dominican Flames said to Ren.

"Get the fuck outta here. I'm good! Like I said, next time, you better come correct."

"Come on, Ren. I need a man like you in my life to love and protect me."

"Yea, right, that'll never happen."

"Aw, that's a'ight, tho'. I got what I wanted," Dominican Flames said, watching the trio of foes walk off.

"What the fuck did she mean, she got what she wanted?" America asked her brother.

"Who knows what that crazy bitch is talkin' 'bout," Ren said.

"Maybe she wanted her guards to get their asses kicked for being dumb enough to fuck with you, bro," C.O. Hooker said with a chuckle.

They all laughed as Ren drove off.

"Get him up! Get him up! Sorry muthafuckas. Y'all lucky y'all ass whoopin' served a greater purpose, or y'all would be left here dead and stinkin'," Dominican Flames told her security guards.

Inside of her SUV, she scrolled down her phone to Monte Bucks' number, and pressed send. After a couple rings, he answered, "Hello, Monte Bucks here."

"Monte, this is Dominican. I got some exclusive footage fo' you, sure to boost ratings. Not even TMZ can get their hands on this," Dominican Flames said, looking at the dashcam mounted in her truck.

"Sounds interesting," Monte Bucks said, sitting up in his bed, and turning his night lap on.

"Oh, it's very interesting."

"That's what I'm talkin' 'bout. Hey, you ready for tomorrow?" Monte said, asking Dominican Flames if she was ready for the teaser party.

"Hell yea, we all set up, ready to turn up. Did my dad put that together for you?"

"Did he? Ya pops is a real dude."

"He's the realest, but what's up with this footage? I'm tryna get it to you."

"A'ight, let me get up. I'll meet you at the club in an hour." "Sounds good," Dominican Flames said as she hung up her cell phone, and fell back into her plush leather seat.

CHAPTER 16:

THE V.I.P.s

Monte Bucks sat inside of his Maybach, listening to “Maybach Music III”, waiting for his celebrity guests to land on the tarmac. He had flown several artists to Pittsburgh to attend his teaser party. It was being held at Dominican Flames' nightclub, Reflections. Some of the guest celebrities had arrived some hours earlier, and were handled by his assistants, but these two particular mega-stars were arriving on his personal Dassault Falcon 7X Learjet. It was the same kind of Learjet Bill Gates owned. "If it's good enough for Gates, it's good enough for Bucks," he would tell people. He wanted to make sure that his V.I.P. guests traveled in the luxurious standards they were accustomed to.

Sipping on D'USSÉ, and smoking his Chohiba cigar, he looked over the footage Dominican Flames had sold him for sixty thousand dollars, and watching it, he felt that it was worth every dollar.

Leaning back, Monte Bucks looked up at the twinkly celestial ceiling of his Maybach, feeling good about what his cast of artist had to offer the world. Then he was alerted of a message that contained a TMZ link. "Fuck!" he blurted out, upset by what he had seen on his iPad. TMZ had gotten their hands on the surveillance footage America had sold him, and he was using some of it for the trailer he was showing at the teaser party.

The funeral was over, the dead had been buried, the blood that stained Reflection's parking lot had been washed away, and business was resuming as usual.

Dominican Flames had put together a red-carpet event to celebrate the first season of *Love & Trap Muzik, Pittsburgh*, and she was premiering the teaser trailer that the producers of the show had them all promoting on their social media pages.

The party was the number one destination to celebrate the fall's upcoming season. More than three thousand guests would be in attendance, including some of the cast members of *Love & Hip Hop, Housewives of Atlanta* and *Empire*.

The invigorating night would spotlight Jay Z's streaming company, Tidal. Jay Z himself was not scheduled to be there, however. "Reality shows ain't my thing," Jay Z told Monte Bucks when asked. Instead, he arranged to send a few of his representatives in his place.

Monte Bucks had tried to get Jay to make an appearance, and when he declined to attend, Monte Bucks sweetened his offer. He wasn't used to hearing no, but after that, if Jay still refused to come, he would not allow his absence to dim the spotlight. Plenty of other improbable mega stars like Kanye West and Kim K, Jeezy, Nicki Minaj, Rick Ross and Drake would light up the event. The night would be star studded, and the cast of *Love & Trap Muzik, Pittsburgh* refused to be outshined.

Outside of the club, exotic cars were being valeted, and a crowd of fans screamed and yelled whenever their favorite celebrity pulled up to the red carpet and exited their steel chariots.

Flashbulbs lit up and camera lenses shuttered as they flickered, lighting up the crowd that surrounded the club's entrance like strobe lights. A man with what seemed to be homosexual tendencies stood on the inside of the entrance with a clipboard in his hand, checking off the invited guests, V.I.P.s, and stars of the hit reality TV show. The red-carpet runway led them inside Reflections. After making it through the flashing lights and sea of screaming fans requesting selfies and autographs, they were greeted by more paparazzi hoopla.

Inside, stars posed for a sequence of pictures in front of a multi-name branded backdrop that displayed the names of sponsors' monikers surrounding the *Love & Trap Muzik, Pittsburgh* name that was printed on its canvas. Hip Hop magazines, entertainment news, bloggers and photographers captured every moment.

Around 7:00 P.M., the LTMP cast members started pulling up. Blocks N Bricks pulled up in a powder blue and cocaine white gutted Bentley Truck. Mr. Frosty Blow pulled behind him in a red Lambo truck; Boom Bap, the legendary female producer, pulled up behind them in a black and yellow Ferrari LaFerrari, sitting on matching colored shoes; Making Hitz pulled up in his BMW i8, and Smack Down and the Smack Dizzy Boyz crept up in two royal blue, silver striped Series II dropped Phantoms. It was like a battle of the ballers affair. Everybody had brought their "A" game.

Then America pulled up in some shit no one had ever seen before. It was a root beer colored, low-slung beast that was all power and speed; a Ronn Motor Company Scorpion that Ronn Maxwell had flown to her from California for the show. As she stepped from behind the Lamborghini doors that opened like a set of wings, all eyes and cameras lit up and were all over her.

"America, America, America!" the crowd yelled. America waved at them and took pictures with some of the fans. She accepted their condolences, but ignored questions about her mother as she made her way to the club.

"Look at'cha girl, Smack. She the flyest thing here," JB said to Smack Down as they turned around to see her taking photographs.

"She shittin' on everybody," Smack Down said as he and his boys walked into Reflections.

After taking pictures for the media, America was mic'd up like the rest of the cast members and escorted to the V.I.P. section.

"Mr. Bucks wants you to share his booth with him," the hostess told her. Two barmaids with sparkling bottles of Ace of Spades followed them to the upper level of the club. The area was kept clear of any riff-raff.

Two huge, muscular men guarding the booth nodded their heads at America. Neither of them were the ones who had fought her brother. One of the huge men unsnapped the velvet rope that blocked the entrance and allowed America to enter the booth.

"Bring me twenty stacks of ones," she told the hostess.

Yeezy Yeezy Yeezy, just jumped over Jumpman

Yeezy Yeezy Yeezy, just jumped over Jumpman

Yeezy Yeezy Yeezy, I feel so accomplished!

I done talked a lot of shit, but I just did numbers

America bobbed her head as Kanye's song "Facts" started playing. Grabbing up a bottle of Ace, she started snaking her head side to side, jerking her body to the beat as she raised her bottle.

If Nike didn't have Drizzy, man, they wouldn't have nothin'

America looked over and saw Drake and the OVO crew in another V.I.P. booth. She smiled when she saw Drake reciting Kanye's lyrics as most of the club was doing. Kanye's *Life of Pablo* CD was the hottest CD on the streets in 2016.

Yeezy Yeezy Yeezy, they line up for days

I ain't drop an album, but the shoes went platinum

Looking around the club, America's eyes widened. She was in total shock and cocked her head back, awestricken. She was fucked up when she saw Kanye in the DJ booth performing the song live, and the LTMP camera crew capturing the live performance.

"2020 I'ma run the whole election," America rapped Kanye's lyrics with him. Popping a Xanny, she chased it with the Ace. She was feeling herself. The night was big.

Towards the end of Kanye's song, Drake made his way to the DJ booth and his crew parted the sea of partygoers for him.

A second LTMF camera crew followed him through the crowd, while other LTMP camera crew filmed Kanye,

America and other cast members while all this was happening. Altogether, there were twelve camera crews recording for the show.

"Nike, Nike, treat employees just like slaves!

Gave Lebron a billi' not to run away," Kanye continued to rap, wrapping his arm around Drake's neck, greeting him, and showing him love. Drake rapped every lyric with him,

then it was his turn. After "Facts", the DJ, DJ Schizo, played Drake and Future's "Jumpman", and Kanye passed the mic to Drake. Drake started rapping his lyrics, zoning out, and doing his dance.

"Jumpman Jumpman Jumpman, them boys up to something

They just spent two or three weeks out the country," Drake rapped.

As Drake rapped, America noticed a big commotion in the crowd. She stopped dancing when she saw what all the commotion was about, and saw who was approaching the V.I.P. booth she was in. It was Dominican Flames and Making Hitz escorting Beyoncé and Jay Z through the club. Monte Bucks and his bodyguard were trailing along them.

America wondered why she was the only one allowed in the booth, and now she knew why. She jumped up and down when she came face to face with the power couple. Beyoncé and Jay Z just smiled at her.

Look at this bitch! She's nothing like her mother. Fuckin' embarrassing, groupie-ass bitch, Dominican Flames thought. Their beef was not over, and she wanted to smack some sense into her, but Monte Bucks had made both of them promise to put their beef to the side for at least a night. He couldn't allow them to fuck up the night over a petty beef. Besides that, he had invested a lot into the night.

"Bitch, I'ma still get at'cha ass. Don't think shit's over between us," Dominican Flames said in America's ear.

"Whatever, bitch!" America replied, not allowing Dominican Flames to ruin her night.

Truth was, America had been around celebrities before. Her mother had introduced her to a lot of them, but none of them were of this magnitude. There were a lot of stars in the building that night, but Beyoncé and Jay Z were on another level.

Seeing them, America was unable to hold her composure. She, like everyone else, was told that Jay Z had been asked to attend the party, but had declined, so to see him and his wife up close and personal was mind blowing.

Again, Monte Bucks had unsuccessfully tried to convince Jay Z to come, but after talking to Dominican Flames about his dilemma, she had spoken to her father about it, and all of a sudden, Jay Z was on board. Come to find out, Dominican Flames' father, Brooklyn Pete, and Jay Z were close friends. So, after he spoke to him, Jay Z called Dominican Flames back personally and assured her that he would be there. So, Dominican Flames was not surprised that he and Beyoncé were there. To her, her father was the real star. He was the one Jay Z spoke highly of, and he was the one who had gotten Jay Z to attend the teaser party. And, not only did Jay Z show up, but he also brought his wife with him.

Beyoncé and Jay Z were used to America's type of reaction to them. As Jay Z maneuvered his way around the V.I.P. booth, Beyoncé held her arms out to give America a welcoming hug.

"Sorry to hear about your family," Beyoncé said, embracing America tightly.

"Thank you, Bey," America responded, breaking their hug, but remaining clasped at the hands.

"Come on, let's have some fun in this bitch!" Beyoncé said.

"You real as shit, Bey," America said, not expecting Beyoncé to be so down to earth.

As Dominican Flames and Monte Bucks discussed what time to show the teaser clip, Beyoncé and Jay Z greeted the other stars who came to their booth to pay homage to the couple worth a billion dollars.

The crowd watched as Rick Ross wrapped his arm around Jay's neck, and Jeezy joked with him, causing him to show that million-dollar smile that only Jay's true friends were familiar with.

"I can't stand that muthafucka. I hate him," Boom Bap said to her girl, gritting on Making Hitz as he mingled with Kanye West. She knew that they were talking about getting together. She had taught him almost everything he knew, she had even opened her legs to him, and a knife in the back was the only thanks she got. Lighting her blunt filled with Khalifa Kush, she put it to her mouth, took a strong pull, and exhaled, never taking her eyes off of the man she still had feelings for.

For America, the night couldn't get any better. She wished her mother was there. She took selfies with Drake, Nicki Minaj, Beyoncé and Jay Z and posted them on her Facebook and Instagram page, captioning it, "A star amongst stars."

Watching her enjoying herself, Smack Down DM'd her and told her how good she looked. They had spoken early that day, and had rescheduled their meeting, but America had reassured him that the money he needed would be there for him whenever he needed it.

"Let's get down to the DJ booth," Monte told Dominican Flames. "We goin' down to the DJ Booth," he also told America. "We about to show the teaser, you ready?" he asked her.

"Yes. Hey, thank you," America said.

"No problem. I told you this was a big opportunity for you. Hey, did you see part of the footage on TMZ? They couldn't show it all; it was too graphic."

"Naaah, I ain't see it. I didn't give it to them."

"Oh, I know you didn't. Someone from the police department did, but we still good. Let me get down here," Monte Bucks said, making his way to the DJ booth.

Once Dominican Flames and Monte entered the DJ booth, DJ Schizo, made an announcement to get the clubgoers' attention, then he gave the mic to Monte Bucks.

"I wanna thank everyone who came out tonight; Beyoncé, Jay Z, Kanye and Kim, Drake, Nicki, Jeezy, Rick Ross, and all the cast members and celebrities in the building. Most of all, I would like to thank Jay Z, his beautiful wife, Beyoncé, and his team at Tidal, and Dominican Flames and her father, Brooklyn Pete, for helping me put this together.

"This year, we're going to show our asses, display a lot of talent, but also address some social issues while also breaking records with TV ratings, right, Dominican?"

"Hell yea," Dominican Flames said, and the crowd went crazy. "Roll that shit," she told the DJ, and huge monitors began to show the teaser for the upcoming season of *Love & Trap Muzik, Pittsburgh*.

As the teaser faded in, you could hear a heartbeat. The inside of a hospital was shown, and someone was being rushed down the hospital hallway on a gurney, and doctors were desperately trying to revive them. Then, there were more heartbeats, and a woman's dying voice was heard saying, "Some kill for power."

The screen flashed to Reflections' parking lot and two jack boys jumped out of their car and approached Sexy Duvall's car with their weapons drawn. One of the jackers started shooting, then the screen fades to black, the heartbeats continue, and the sound of a woman's gravelly voice sounds again. "Through acts of betrayal, infamy is born."

The hospital room, 718, is shown, the heartbeat

continues, and the door to room 718 slowly opens, and the woman's voice continues, "One's last breath leads to another's new beginning."

The heartbeats continue, the screen fades out, then back in, and the cast of *Love & Trap Muzik, Pittsburgh* are seen leaving the church behind a casket being carried by six pallbearers to a line of black hearses and the woman's voice sounds again. "Some rise from the trap to become the most powerful in the industry..." The screen fades out, then back in, the heartbeat continues, and a gravesite is shown. The cast stands at the gravesite and America steps forward and drops a black rose onto the casket as it is lowered into the ground, and the screen fades to black.

The heartbeat continues, and the cast members are seen divided on each sides of a stage, walking towards the two golden microphones facing each other on the spotlighted stage. The woman's voice sounds again, "Us, we run shit for the love of our city..." The cast members continue to walk towards the two gold microphones and America and Mr. Frosty Blow grab a microphone from each side, and the entire cast turns towards the camera.

The screen fades out and returns showing the inside of room 718. The camera slowly pans up the body of the person laying in the hospital bed, and finally, Sexy Duvall's bandaged face is revealed. Her eyes are closed, the screen fades out, heartbeats are heard, then the screen fades back in to Sexy Duvall with her eyes open, and she says in a dying voice, "Welcome to Pittsburgh!" The title, *Love & Trap Muzik, Pittsburgh*, is shown on the screen, and the screen fades out.

The audience erupts, and Dominican Flames and Monte Bucks hug. His business partner, Money King, wasn't there, but he streamed the event for her. Due to her physical condition, she mostly played the background. It wasn't that she was ashamed of being paraplegic, she just didn't like a lot of attention.

"Ma, they loved it. That shit was so tight. Yea, go to the LTMP website to see it; Mr. Bucks live streamed it," America said to her mother. Looking over the crowd of applause, America and Dominican Flames' eyes locked. It was clear that their beef wasn't over, regardless of how good the teaser was. Dominican Flames couldn't wait until America saw the other footage. She was sure that she wouldn't like the fact that she had sold her brother's street footage for a hefty price.

Rolling her eyes and turning her head from looking at America, Dominican Flames turned back to a smiling Monte Bucks with a fake smile on her face, and joined in on the applause. It was hard, but she took in the night without beefing or lashing out. Monte had made it clear that the night was to be drama-free or someone would be cut from the show. With the footage and the night's takeaway, she stood to make at least a quarter of a million dollars. Bottle sales alone had made her over a hundred thousand dollars, but she still planned on getting revenge because betrayal was something that she didn't tolerate.

In the movies, when a baller made a massive drug deal, it would take place at some kind of warehouse. The supplier would be surrounded by shady Uzi-toting goons lurking in every shadow, and the baller would always demand to see the product before coughing up the money. But, with Smack Down, that wasn't the case. After doing business with each other for close to a decade, he and his connect had built a bond, and fully trusted one another, so neither of them needed back up. Though, they had never seen each other during a transaction. They both believed that the less people involved, the better. But knowing something could go wrong at any given time, they still took precautions.

The money was exchanged at least a week before, the drugs were delivered safely to an unknown place, and then a text was sent to Smack Down, detailing the drugs' whereabouts.

Over the years, they had developed a step-by-step process of doing things. Using this strategy, they had never been jacked or investigated, as far as they knew.

Smack Down would send the money, his connect's most trusted middleman would drop the work off at a motel used by semi-truck drivers, then JB or Smack Down would pick the work up and cut and stash it until it was ready to be delivered or sold. In almost ten years, nothing had changed, and everything ran smoothly. All the players remained the same, but this time, there would be an addition to the team. If America came through with her five hundred thousand dollars, she would be an equal partner, and they would be copping more work than he ever had. As long as he stayed in charge, and she didn't disrupt his effective way of doing things, he was cool with that.

****

The day after the teaser party, Smack Down drove to America's estate, thinking about the time he had jacked

Mar Mar and his connect at a place similar to hers. It was 5:30 A.M. when he called her from her driveway. He was surprised when she answered his call on the first ring. She had told him that she had been up since five o'clock, waiting for his call. Less than a minute later, she came to the door, and waved him in.

"New car, huh?" America asked Smack Down, holding the door open for him. He walked past, looking back at the 2001 Windstar he did his dirt in.

"Yea, I'm tryna impress you," he told her.

"Hmph! You already did. Come up to my room," she said to him with a smile on her face.

"How you feelin'?" Smack Down asked, watching America's ass sway back and forth in her thin, Mickey Mouse-printed pajama pants as he followed her up her steps.

Inside her room, Ren finished rubber banding the five hundred thousand dollars that was sprawled across the bed. "What up?" he said, greeting Smack Down.

“Sup, fam?" Smack Down replied.

"Let's put the money in this bag," America suggested, taking an overnight bag out of her closet, and throwing it on her bed.

"How much is this?" Smack Down asked as he helped throw stacks of money into the bag.

"Five hunnid stacks. Ain't that what you asked fo'? How much am I gon' make back?" America asked, uncertain of her return. She wanted to make things clear.

Ren looked up, waiting for Smack Down's answer as he helped them throw more money into the bag.

"First of all, of course I'm going to match you, so we goin' in wit' a mill ticket. Now, let me show you what ya return is gon' be," Smack Down said as he pulled out his cell phone, and went to its calculator. "At twenty racks a brick, we'll get fiddy bricks for a mill'. I'll turn that into seventy-five of them thangs, and..." Smack Down punched 75x32,000 into the calculator, and pressed the equal sign and $2,400,000 popped up on the LCD screen.

"Two point four mill', that's what I'm talkin' 'bout! You hear that, bruh?" America asked Ren.

Ren put his head down as he threw the last of the stacks into the overnight bag, acting like he wasn't paying attention to what they were talking about or doing.

"Nah, what's that, sis'?" he asked, but Smack Down peeped his game. There was something Smack Down wasn't feeling about him, and that shady move really made him feel uncomfortable around Ren. He didn't like fake-ass niggas.

"He said we gon' make 2.4 million off this deal right here."

"That's what's up," Ren said, zipping the huge bag up, and handing it to Smack down. "Sis', you tell him yet?" Ren asked.

"Oh, yea, Smack, my brother need five of my ki's. He got a sale fo' 'em," America revealed.

"Aaagh," Smack Down expressed, a little

reluctantly.

"Fam, I been doin' this. My people can't go without just because you came aboard," Ren said, making it seem like his sister was doing Smack Down a favor when, in fact, Smack Down was doing them justice. But, five kilos was nothing. Smack Down would really be getting seventy-

five kilos, and stretching them into a hundred and twenty-five bricks. So, her cut wouldn't change, but instead of 1.2 million dollars, he would be making 2.8 million.

"I feel you. I'll make my move and text you afterwards and tell you where to come and pick ya five up."

"Cool," Ren replied, shaking his head in agreement.

"Thanks again, Smack," America said, putting her arms out for a hug. As Smack Down went to hug America, he looked down at her hard nipples pointing out through her wife beater. Seeing him checking out her breasts, she embraced him tightly for a few seconds. She was letting him know that she wanted him to do more than just look.

"Ayo, thanks for yesterday. You know, lookin' out fo' my sister. I don't know what I would've done without her," Ren said, wrapping his arm around America's neck.

"No doubt. Now, let me get outta here, and get on this. I need to switch my order to fifty before they get in motion," Smack Down said, picking up the hefty bag filled with street money.

"Damn, ya man got it like that? On deck like that?"

Ren asked, his thoughts spilling into words.

"Hell yea, we good," Smack Down replied, hating everything about Ren.

"Let me walk you out," America said.

Outside, America hugged Smack Down again. This time, she gave him a kiss on the cheek after hugging him. "Please, be careful. I don't want nothin' to happen to you."

"I'm good," Smack Down said, putting the night bag filled with five hundred thousand dollars into the van. Then he walked around to the driver side, jumped in the van, and rolled down the passenger side window.

"I'm just makin' sure you watch yaself. Ya my new money getta, my new Jigga."

"Oh, yea?" Smack Down laughed.

"Yea, and I'm ya Bey."

"Yeeaah, okay." Smack Down felt a similar connection to her. It reminded him of what he and Money had early in their relationship. "I'll be a'ight. This is what I do."

"Hit me when everything is done. Maybe we can get together for a drink or some'in'. Do it fo' the show, or fo' real," America took her shot.

"Everything I do is fo' real. Anyway, I don't know about goin' out wit' you. You gotta stalker hittin' you up wit' paintballs an' shit," Smack Down said jokingly, starting up his van.

"Yea right, quit playin' wit' me. That bitch don't want no mo' problems. Especially after last night."

"What happened last night? You mean to tell me some mo' action took place after I dropped ya ass off?" Smack Down asked, leaning towards the passenger side.

"Yeeeaaah! My brother beat the shit outta the two bodyguards that hit me up."

"Get the fuck outta here!"

"Hell yea!"

"Yo! Please tell me you ain't tell him 'bout that body."

"I tell him everything. We don't keep secrets from each other."

"Aw, man, what the fuck!"

"But he ain't gon' say shit. That nigga put in work, too. He was in the military. How you think that nigga who shot my moms ended up dead in the county?"

"I seen that shit on the news. He did that shit?"

America gazed at Smack Down for a couple seconds. "He had it done."

"Daaamn! That reminds me, I gotta deal wit' that body in the studio," Smack Down said, cold and casual like murder was nothing to him. He was remorseless. "What you doin' today?" he asked.

"I gotta go pick my moms up. She get out today, and I know she wanna know about everything that's goin' on."

“So you gon' tell her, too, huh? Shit's crazy," Smack Down said, shaking his head.

"If I don't, my brother will. Nigga, we ain't no rats! You good. You saved my life. My people ain't gon' come at you wit' no snitch shit!" America said, starting to get frustrated, realizing she might have fucked up her chances of getting with Smack Down because of loose lips.

She knew that niggas didn't like nosy bitches, or bitches who ran their mouths, especially about murder.

"It's cool. I ain't trippin'," Smack Down lied. He was very discreet about his street affairs. Money didn't even know about every move he had made. Now he wondered if saving her was worth it.

"I couldn't tell my moms shit in the hospital because she thought everything was bugged.”

"Damn, she paranoid like that?"

"I told you we know all ’bout the game. Our shit is all the way on point."

"You don't know nothin'," Smack Down said, pulling off

with a chuckle.

"Be safe, my lil Jigga," she taunted him.

"Ha, whatever," Smack Down replied.

"You really like that nigga, huh?" Ren asked, stepping out of the house and onto the driveway.

"Yea, I do."

"Hopefully he do the right thing. I would hate to have to kill the nigga, you know, bein' that you like him."

"Shit, bro, business is business. He fuck up, he gotta die. Until then, I fucks wit' him hard body."

Ren got into his car and pulled off, leaving America thinking in the driveway.

America also gave Smack Down some things to think about. He thought about killing the whole Duvall household. He didn't like the fact that they knew about what he did. Then he thought about what proof they would have. "None!" he said out loud, and shook the thought of killing America out of his head. He thought about her brother beating down Dominican Flames' bodyguards. *Them some big niggas,* he thought. *Nigga's a five-brick headache. All in the fuckin' way!*

I'll have JB bring him his five joints after we cut it up. Should I do it before or after I do the big deal? Nah, can't risk the bulk of the weight. I don't know what this clown's up to. We'll do it after we put up everything, just in case he tries something."

****

AT THE HOME OF DETECTIVE CASTANEDA GORDY

Detective Gordy answered her cell phone, groggy and half-asleep. "Hello?"

"Get up. We gotta stiff in a studio on McKnight Road. Looks like the victim is linked to that reality TV show based in Pittsburgh. It's as though someone is targeting the cast members of the show."

"This would be the second shooting victim that is part of the show. Did you call the producers of the show and see if he had beef with anybody?"

"Yup, before I called you. I talked to our inside person there."

"Good. So, the camera people are there already, I assume?" Detective Gordy was speaking about Money King's camera crew. The two detectives had made a deal with her. They were to give her any firsthand information involving the show in exchange for money. With Sexy's case closed, the detectives saw another opportunity that involved the new victim of the show. The call made to Money King would make them a pretty penny.

WE TRAP OR DIE 174

As Detective Gordy finished washing her face, her partner called again. "Yea, Ray?" she said, answering her cell phone.

"Today's our lucky day. Another body, and guess what?" "It's tied to *Love &Trap Muzik, Pittsburgh*?"

"Yup."

"You gotta be kidding," Detective Gordy said, checking her dark complected face for any cole that may have been left in the corners of her eyes.

"Nope. It's no joke. It's the third stiff tied to the show," Detective Burnam answered."

"Let me guess, you already made the call to Money

King?" Detective Gordy asked with a chuckle.

"Yup. They're sending a second camera crew to the crime scene. You head over there, I'll take this one."

"Where am I going?"

"Three-one-nine Balboa," Detective Burnam gave Detective Gordy the address to the home of the third victim related to the LTMP show.

BASS-LINE RECORDING STUDIO, 1021 MCKNIGHT ROAD, Detective Burnam said to a medical examiner technician, "What are we looking at here? Run me through it."

"Execution-style murder. Two to the back of the head. The first one collapsed the victim, and the second shot was to make sure the victim was dead," the tech told the detective.

"Typical street-thug killin', or do you think it was a contract murder?"

"Shit, it's hard to say nowadays. These kids are watching movies or doing what they see on TV or video games, and they're leaving no witnesses. They have that make-sure-he's-dead mentality," the tech said, looking at the remains of Carson "Hitter B." Wells.

"Detective Burnam took notes as the tech was talking.

The soundboard, notepad and soundproof walls were all covered with skull and brain fragments. A shiny black vinyl body bag laid unzipped next to Hitter B., awaiting his cold, lifeless body.

Technicians methodically took pictures, blood samples, and documented everything worth value on the scene.

LTMP cameramen videotaped what they were allowed to. Monte Bucks planned to get the pictures and footage of Hitter B.'s body at the morgue. He had contacted Hitter B.'s family, and propositioned them. He would take care of all funeral expenses in exchange for photos of the body.

Detectives Burnam and Gordy also accepted fees for inside information about the murders, and were to make statements for the show.

"Give me something," Detective Burnam said in an emotionless monotone to another tech taking pictures of the murder scene.

"It's a lot going on here, but what I can say for now is that this was a well thought out murder. At one point, the floor was covered with something, and the victim trusted whoever shot him—"

"Hold up, you said the floor was covered?" Detective Burnam asked, making sure he had heard the tech correctly.

"Yes. You have blood on the soundboard and notepad; everything but the floor. The way this man's body is positioned is not how it was when it first hit the floor. Put it this way; whoever shot him, placed something underneath the victim before shooting him, possibly a sheet of plastic or something. And after they shot him, instead of rolling the body up and moving it, the killer pulled whatever the material was from underneath the victim, causing him to roll into the position we found him in."

"So, I need to check every garbage bin in the vicinity?" Detective Burnam asked.

"For starters," the tech said, taking a few more pictures of Hitter B.'s body. These were for billionaire, Monte Bucks; he was also on his payroll.

"Wow!" Detective Burnam shook his head as he wrote down a few notes. "Let me continue to gather what I can and I'll keep you informed," the tech told the detective.

"Please do."

"Oh! But let me remind you that this is a studio, so there will be a lot of DNA samples of innocent people rendered. People walk in and out of here a thousand times a dat, so get ready to do a lot of work," the tech advised in between taking snapshots of the dead body.

****

AT THE SECOND CRIME SCENE, 319 BALBOA ST.

Detective Gordy had to fight through the small crowd of uniformed officers, news crew. lights, cameras and spectators, she scribbled her initials on a line of the crime scene attendance log, and ducked under the yellow crime scene tape.

Placing her Ulyana Sergeenko hand embroidered sunglasses on top of her head, she held the back of her hand to her mouth and nose. The stench of the dead body was strong. "Anything good for me?" she asked a medical examiner technician, watching another dusting the fingerprint powder onto the knob of the front door of the victim's home.

"Victim's cell phone's been ringing nonstop."

Beep! Beep! Beep!

A message alerted. Detective Gordy looked at the LCD screen on the phone; it showed fifty-nine missed calls.

"What else?" Detective Gordy asked.

"Hispanic, male, 62", forty-five years of age. Victim died between 3:30 and 4:30 A.M. Body found in the living room area at approximately 8:30 A.M., this morning when the girlfriend got off work. Cause of death: single shot, close range, center forehead. Guy's face completely unrecognizable. The left eye blown out. No shell casing left behind indicates that the killer was a work for hire. With positive identification from the girlfriend, and ID in his wallet, we're sure the victim is Pedro Sanchez. We found a security pass; victim was the head of security for Reflections nightclub."

Pedro's cell phone vibrated, and alerted that a message had been received. Detective Gordy picked it up again; this time, she pressed menu on the phone, and selected text message.

TEXT MESSAGE:

WHERE THE FUCK ARE YOU? the text message read.

Detective Gordy pressed on the number highlighted above the message box, and it automatically dialed the number the text message was sent from. After a couple rings, she heard a female's voice yelling into the phone, "Where the fuck are you, Pedro?" Dominican Flames yelled into the receiver.

Pulling the phone away from her ear, Detective Gordy checked the LCD screen and it read: Dominican. "Hello?" the detective answered.

"Who this?" Dominican Flames asked with firmness in her voice.

"Detective Castaneda Gordy from Pittsburgh's Robbery-Homicide Division."

"What are you doin' wit' Pedro's... NO! NO! NO!" Dominican Flames asked, then she figured out what happened to Pedro.

"Something bad has happened to Pedro. Can we meet and talk?"

"NOOOO!" Dominican Flames wailed into the phone.

"Ma'am... Ma'am, please, where are you located?"

"Oh no, Pedro. Pedro!"

"Ma'am, where are you? Where can we meet, Dominican?" "Wait! How do you know my name?"

"It's in Pedro's contact's. Where can I meet you?"

"Um, I'm at Reflections in the Strip District."

"Okay, I'm on my way. I have a few questions."

"Okay, anything you need. I'll be here. Does his family know yet?"

"We'll talk when I get there."

"A'ight," Dominican said, pressing end to disconnect the phone call, then she wiped the fake tears from her face. They were only a part of the great performance she was about to give veteran homicide detective, Gordy. She'd had Pedro killed because of the breach in her security, and the leak of security footage, but she was going to make sure the detective did not suspect her or the murder.

****

AT THE DUVALL ESTATE

America and Ren helped their mother into the house, up the steps, and into her bedroom. Inside were flowers, balloons, gifts, and get-well cards. "Ren, get this shit outta here!"

"Ma." America couldn't believe what she was hearing from her mother's mouth. She thought that she would be happy to see all the love people had for her.

"America, I'm sick of looking at this type of shit. All it does is remind me of that damn hospital, and that I've been shot the fuck up. I don't need to look at this shit fo' that. I got all these bullet wounds and scars fo' that!"

"Calm down, Ma. I got you. I understand. Let's just get you into the bed, and Ren will get this stuff outta here," America said.

"Yea. I got you, Ma," Ren said as he started removing the gifts.

"Thank you, baby. Ugh, shiiit! This shit hurts. I feel like the bride of Frankenstein. Did DQ send me anything?" Sexy Duvall asked, settling into bed.

"I thought you didn't want that stuff, Ma," America said with a smirk on her face.

"Bitch! Did he send me some'in' or not?" Sexy Duvall asked again, smiling back at her daughter.

"Yes, Ma. He sent you some'in'."

"What?"

"He sent the ten dozen roses right there." America pointed to the roses. "You wanna read the card?" she asked her mother.

"Yes, I wanna read the card. Let me see it. Agh, shit!" Sexy Duvall felt the pain up and down her body every time she moved, and the pain was written all over her face.

"It saaaysss..." America pretended she was going to read the card.

"I can read it! Let me see," Sexy Duvall demanded.

The card read:

To the realest chick I know,

Love you, and I can't wait till you fully recover so you can get back to runnin' shit!

Love, DQ

Sexy Duvall smiled as she gave America back the card. "Rennnn!" she called out to her son.

"Yea, Ma?" he answered.

"I want some Olive Garden. You feel like gettin' me some?"

"Yea. I got you, Ma. What you want?" Ren asked, stepping back into his mother's bedroom to remove more of her flowers and gifts.

"Get me a Tour of Italy. You can get the rest of this shit later. I'm tryna eat."

“A’ight. I'll be right back," he said, kissing his

mother's forehead. "Love you," he said, leaving to go get her food.
"Love you, too, soldier," Sexy Duvall said, calling Ren by the nickname she had given him since he had joined the military.

"You want anything, A?" Ren asked America.

"Nah, I'm good, bro. Ma, you want anything else while we wait to get ya food?" she asked her mother.

"A glass of wine and a blunt," Sexy Duvall said with a serious look on her face.

"Maaaa?"

"Americaaa. Don't play, bitch. Roll the fuck up. I need something to take my mind off his pain."

"Okay, I got you."

"Where's my phone at? Did the lawyer get it back?"

"Yea, I got it in the safe. Mr. Bucks got some serious mouthpieces on his payroll. Our lawyer couldn't get it back but his lawyer made one phone call, and they released it back to us."

"Yea, Monte got a lot of power. He's the most powerful black man in Pittsburgh, legal-wise, and one of the most powerful men in the entertainment industry."

"Shit! He cut a million-dollar check like it wasn't shit. Made me think I should've asked fo' mo'."

"I know that's right, baby girl."

"Fo' real. Let me get ya stuff fo' you, Ma. You wanna see the pictures from the teaser party?" America asked, walking out of her mother's bedroom, and into hers.

"Yea. Bring them, too. I loved the teaser. Agh,"

Sexy Duvall said, adjusting herself into a comfortable position.

"Yea, we killed it. We got over forty million YouTube views," America yelled from her room.

The combination buttons beeped as she punched in her code on the electric keypad that was hidden behind a large family portrait, hanging on her bedroom wall. Inside was two hundred thousand dollars, her mother's cell phone inside of a sealed evidence bag, and her mother's black book and payment ledgers. Locking the safe back, she grabbed the teaser party pictures from her dresser, and headed back to her mother's bedroom. Before she did, she checked for her Lanvin Bag and took it with her.

"I brought ya black book and ledger, too, and here's ya phone." America sat everything on her mother's bed.

"Thank you, princess. I know them trick-ass muthafuckas was goin' crazy when they thought I was goin' to die. You know ya moms got the best pussy on planet earth, and it's expensive."

"Ma, you are crazy!"

"America, roll up!" Sexy Duvall demanded. She had not smoked a blunt since she had gotten shot. "Aaagh, A, be careful!" America had caused her mother pain as she climbed onto her bed.

"Sorry, Ma," America said, digging into her purse and pulling a baby food jar filled with Sour Diesel out of it.

Sexy Duvall opened the packet of pictures, and took them out of a picture envelope. The first picture she saw was a picture of America, Beyoncé and Jay Z. "Damn!" she expressed disappointment.

"What, Ma?" America asked, filling a blunt wrap with Sour.

"I'm mad as hell I couldn't be there."

"Yea, I wish you could have been there, too." America licked the blunt leaf, and tightly wrapped it around the Sour.

"Shit! Jay and Bey! I would've gotten into their bed for free."

"You crazy, Ma," she said as she lit the blunt, took a few puffs, and passed it to her mother, blowing smoke into the air.

“I see y’all was kickin’ drip,” Sexy Duvall said, using some new slang she had heard her kids using.

"Shut up, Ma. They some real muthafuckas, tho’."

"They gettin' paper, too," Sexy Duvall said, going through the pictures closely.

"I got me a money getta."

"Bitch! Who?"

"Smack Down!"

"Girl, you can't handle that nigga. Besides that, that's my girl's baby daddy, and she's the one who hired you to be on the show. Do you really wanna play yaself like that?" Sexy Duvall gave her daughter something to think about. "I need to call Money. That's my bitch. I'll cut'cha ass off 'bout her."

"Whatever!" America rolled her eyes at her mother.

"You think because he saved ya life, and he's flippin' ya money that he's yours, but he's always gonna be Money's. She lost her legs because of him. That's why him and Frosty don't get along."

"Why, Ma?" America wanted the tea on Smack Down and the executive producer of the show, Ms. Money King.

"Smack Down got Money caught up in a jack move he did, and she got shot by the brother of the dude they jacked. Then Frosty shot Smack, and tried to kill him."

"What?"

"Hell yea. They wanted to put Frosty in jail, but Smack Down wouldn't testify against him. So, you know, he a stand-up nigga. But, like I was saying, he dedicated his life to her. Look, I don't wanna tell you he's outta ya league, but princess, he's outta ya league. Shit, I wouldn't be surprised if that work you coppin' today was comin' from her. She been gettin' money, and had her own connect since her

and Smack did that jack. Fo' real, fo' real, this is her fuckin' show."

"Damn, I ain't know all of that," America said, watching her mother pull on the blunt, going through the pictures. "Whew, is that nigga that kidnapped you in here?" Sexy Duvall asked. She wanted to see the dead man who had kidnapped her daughter.

"Yea, let me see." America took the stack of pictures and flipped through them until she came to a picture of Smack Down and the late Hitter B.

"Shut up, bitch! Shut up fo' I kill ya ass!" America flinched. She could still hear his voice as she relived the ordeal in her head.

"That's him?" Sexy Duvall asked.

"Yea, that's him," America answered with tears in her eyes.

"Aw, princess, you ain't gotta worry 'bout him no mo', he's gone. What I'm worried about is you and Dominica. We need to put an end to y'all feud. If she gotta beef, it should be with me, not you. Her security sold you the footage on the strength of me. What's her new number?"

"Let me get it outta my phone. I don't know it by heart," America said, extending her arm to her mother with the blunt in her hand. "Here, you want this?"

"Nah, I'ma roll another one. I can't believe you and Dominica are beefin'. That bitch is supposed to be our manager," Sexy Duvall said, going through the call log of her phone.

As she did so, message alerts kept popping up on her LCD screen. "FUCK! These damn messages keep poppin' up," she said. Then she paused when she saw the number of her jacker still in her phone.

"Fuck that bitch. She ain't my fuckin' manager, you are. Here go her number."

"Dial it."

"She might not answer when she sees my number."

"You right, let me see the number. I'll call her from my number. She'll definitely answer that."

America's phone vibrated. "Hello? Two people? When? That's crazy. I'm sorry to hear that," America spoke on her cell phone, and Sexy Duvall spoke into hers. "Hello? Hi, Dominica. I'm glad to be home. Look, we need to get together and talk. A detective, fo' what? Oh, okay. That's crazy. Call me as soon as you can. Love you, too." Sexy Duvall called Dominica so she could kill the beef between the two girls who had grown up like sisters, but Dominica was sitting with Detective Gordy, so she told her to stop by the club around 9:00 P.M., and she would set up a conference call between her and her incarcerated parents.

"Sounds good. We'll be here at the house," America told her caller.

"It's show time fo' you. That was the cameraman from the show. They tryna get some footage. They want to reenact you coming home from the hospital."

"Shit, they better do it here 'cause I ain't goin' back to the hospital," Sexy Duvall said as her message alert sounded.

"Nah, they're just gonna get you gettin' outta the car, coming into the house, and a few other shots."

“A’ight, that's cool. Speaking of gettin' outta the car, you was tellin' me about a lil scuffle Soldier got into last night. He didn't shoot anyone, did he?"

"Nah, he just beat the shit outta that bitch's security guards, but the cameraman was tellin' me about two men associated with cast members being shot and killed last night. We both know one was my kidnapper, but guess who the other one was?"

"Who?"

"Pedro, that guard who sold us the footage."

"WHAT? See, that's why this beefin' shit gotta end. I'm already dealin' wit' losing ya grandma, and I'm not tryna lose you or ya brother over no bullshit ’cause the Grouch goes hard. That's prolly who got Pedro killed. She can make those kinda calls from her jail cell."

CHAPTER 17:

WHO GOT THE JUICE

AT THE FEMALE CORRECTIONAL CENTER IN HAZELTON, WV

Giselle "El Grunona" Duarte stood on the second tier of her cell block with a few of her female goons around her. She was the shot caller of the Latin Americans in the facility. She and her husband, Peter "Brooklyn Pete" Duarte, had been locked up for over two decades. Giselle's long stay in prison had kept her angry, mad and bitter, and that was why they called her Grunona; it meant grouch in Spanish. At first, her friends called her that in secrecy, and when she found out about the nickname, she was furious about it. But, her husband found it cute, so she grew to accept it.

Grunona gazed out at the cells and inmates surrounding her and felt sick. She was sick of doing time. Sick of watching the same activities taking place every day; card playing, dominoes games, working out and watching the same TV programs.

It was six o'clock, and she and her bandilleras stood where they did everyday around that time. They were waiting for mail-call. La Patrona de Patronas and her mafia, La Senoras del Bandidas, watched as the C.O. running the block walked into the unit with the mail carrier pouch, and yelled out, "Mail-call!" He poured the mail out onto a table in the unit. After a few seconds, he picked pieces of mail up, and started calling out names. "Balvin, Palmer, Santos, Duarte, Duarte, Duarte, Duarte." The inmate who ran the block for her, Kieko Silverio, grabbed

Grunona's mail and brought it to her.

"Gracias," Grunona told her right-hand bitch, accepting her mail.

"What time you want ya phone?" Kieko asked the lady O.G.

"Right after nine o'clock count."

"Some chica named Sexy left you a message. She said she needs to talk to you about the girls." Kieko was talking about a message Sexy had left on Grunona's illegal cell phone.

"Okay, I'll hit her back later. I'ma go lay down for a minute."

"Okay. I got the our chicas baggin' up the work, and we should be ready to distribute it tonight."

"Good. Stay on top of it. Who works tonight?"

"Ms. Bradley."

Grunona nodded her head and went into her cell to relax. Inside of her cell, Grunona sat on her bunk and went through her mail. She had several pieces; two cards from Dominica, an envelope of pictures from the teaser party, *New York Times, Pittsburgh Courier* and a *Vanity Affair* with Monte Bucks on the cover.

Laying back in her bunk, Grunona picked up the *Vanity Affair* and flipped through the pages until she saw the article on the executive of the reality show her daughter was a part of. She had heard about Monte Bucks, but knew little about him. She hoped the article would enlighten her about the billionaire her daughter worked for.

As Grunona read about Monte Bucks and his wealth, she began to daydream. She envisioned herself in a boardroom, two million-dollar cars and a plush penthouse overlooking Pittsburgh's skyline. Snapping out of her fantasy, she read the Q&A part of the interview.

VA: So, what can we expect from Season One of *Love & Trap Muzik, Pittsburgh*?

MB: A lot of entertainment! A lot of action. Live footage from a murder investigation, performances from the cast members and mega-stars. The whole works. We're bringing it on another level.

VA: Thirty years in the industry is a long time. Have you ever thought about publishing a memoir?

MB: That's actually in the works. One of the guys from the show, DQ Dawg, is co-writing it with me. We just started our publishing company, Bucks Baby Publishing. He ran the idea pass me, and I was all for it. I feel it's time for me to tell my story.

VA: You were part of the group Status in the eighties, and found success with the group, but due to financial differences, the group split. Have you ever thought about doing a reunion tour?

MB: To date, Status has sold 20 million records. We could have sold 100 million, but it wasn't meant to be. We all moved on. A reunion, I doubt it. It's not in the plans. We've had private sessions, but that's just something I'm not interested in.

VA: Shortly after the split, you started your own record label, Chalice Recordings, but in 1997, you sold your part of the company, and walked away from the music business. Why was that?

MB: I felt like the music industry was declining, so I walked away while I was still on top. A state of independence was on the rise.

Artists like Puffy, Jay Z, Cash Money Records, Aftermath and several others were coming in the game to reset the scoreboard, so I just got outta their way. I felt that my era in the music industry had run its course.

VA: You quit during the time some would say was the golden era of the industry, 1988-2003, but you didn't stop developing artists. Some of the artist you just mentioned are some of the artist you helped become successful. Do you take responsibility for that?

MB: That's a tricky question because how do you take claim to that? How do you take responsibility for the success of an artist who's already successful? Yes, I've given a lot of advice to upcoming artist. I've given them advice at 3:00 A.M., and I still do. Me and Puff have spent hours discussing the future of Hip Hop, but I'm not looking for a pat on the back. I'm not asking an hourly fee. I'm not a bloodsucking executive. I just tell them what I believe is the best for them at the time.

VA: Is that what you do with the cast members of LTMP?

MB: That's exactly how I handle things with my family members. *Love & Trap Muzik, Pittsburgh* is a show I co-created with my partner, Money King. We've created an outlet for young artist to display their talent, but their drive, their story, makes millions of viewers relate to them, and that's what makes them successful. It's just my advice and guidance that keeps them successful.

"Patrona, Patrona, they just showed it on the news. Pedro is dead. We got him." Kieko ran to Grunona's cell to tell her that the hit she had put out on the security guard who had crossed her daughter had been carried out.

Grunona sat back and closed her eyes. She thought about the day she would run a Fortune 500 company, and make the Forbes list like Monte Bucks.

CHAPTER 18:

MONEY & POWER

On the way to the Reflection Night Club, Sexy Duvall spoke to Giselle Duarte in Spanish. "I know, girl. I'm sorry 'bout how that shit got handled," Sexy Duvall said.

"And before it comes out, I have to let you know that Dom recorded Ren's street brawl and sold it to the show. She's crazy. I don't understand what's going on with these two. They were raised as sisters," Grunona said.

"It's this damn reality TV shit. I smoothed that out with A and Monte—"

"Monte Bucks?"

"Yea, his ass. Talkin' 'bout he's glad they deadin' the beef. He said he got homicide detectives breathing down his neck, and protesters threatening to shut the show down. It's crazy, girl."

"Homicide detectives? One was asking Dom questions earlier. What are they sayin' to Monte?"

"Nothin' much. They think that some sicko is runnin' around killin' reality show muthafuckas."

"What? Everybody's crazy out there. Maybe I should stay my ass in here, girl."

"Yea right, bitch! I need ya ass out here!" Sexy Duvall said to her close friend. Just like their daughters, they had grown up calling each other sisters. For Grunona, laughing was out of the norm. Hearing her playfully joke was not something her bandilleras were used to. Giselle had earned her nickname, "The Grouch," honestly. And, for someone to call her bitch was completely unheard of inside the Federal Correctional Center. Many had died for lesser. Your tone of voice could get you killed dealing with her. There was only one person she feared and submitted to, and that was her husband, Brooklyn Pete. She wasn't nearly as bloodthirsty and powerful as he was.

"So, when are they lettin' yo' ass outta there?" Sexy Duvall asked.

"Me and Pete just put in for clemency again. Obama has been showing love. He let close to two hundred people go so far, so we're hoping that our case hits his desk, and he releases us."

"I'ma holla at Monte fo' y'all. You know he played a big part in gettin' Obama elected. He's always at one of Obama's functions."
"Oh yea? That sounds great. Please do."

America's cell phone rung as her mother and Giselle spoke. It was her brother. "What's up, brother?"

"Hey, I'm on my way to meet'cha man," Ren told America.

"By yaself, right?" America asked.

"Come on, A. Of course, I'm by myself."

"By yaself, right!" America said again, catching her mother's eye. They were simultaneously having conversations.

"Hey, baby, I'm almost at the club," Sexy Duvall

said to Giselle.

"Yea, A, by myself." Ren wanted to take Hooker, but America told had him that would alarm Smack Down.

"We're going to FaceTime Pete. He wants to talk to the girls together," Sexy Duvall said to Giselle.

"Good! He'll make 'em kiss and make up fo' sure," Giselle replied.

"Bye, brother. Call me when you make it back safe," America said to Ren, ending their conversation.

"They better kiss and make up and quit tryna mess their money up. I'm sick of funding America's purse and car fetish."

"Fo' real, girl. We had to get Dom that damn club. She was deep in our pocket's."

"I hear that. Hey, we're pullin' up. I'll call you soon. And I will definitely holla at Monte fo' you and Pete. Shit, I'ma do whatever I have to do to get y 'all out. Even if I gotta suck the president's dick or have a threesome with him and Michelle's fine ass. You know I will."

Giselle laughed with Sexy Duvall. "Bitch, do whatever you gotta do, just get us outta this bitch!"

"I got y'all. Hey, I'm gone. Love you wit' everything in me, senora del bandida."

"Love you, too, doll face," Grunona said, pressing end on her smartphone.

As she leaned back, Kieko watched her boss, and

after a few seconds, she asked, "Who was that?"

"One of the realest bitches I've ever known in my life," Grunona answered.

CHAPTER 19:

UNFINISHED BUSINESS

Ren had just pulled into the parking lot of the Pittsburgh Inn on Route 65. Little did he know, he was being tailed by two money-hungry detectives, Gordy and Burnam. They had already made fifty thousand dollars that day, and were looking to make more. The more money they made from providing information to Monte Bucks, the more they wanted. It was easy money.

After making the fifty thousand dollars, Burnam came up with an idea. *"Why don't we put the cast members of LTMP under surveillance? All these luxury cars, diamonds and mansions, somebody gotta be doin' something illegal. Instead of just bustin' they asses, and them paying hundreds of thousands of dollars on legal fees, why don't we arrest them and make Monte Bucks pay for us to release them without a charge?" he had suggested to his partner.*

Detective Gordy thought it was a great idea, and was all for it, so they searched Facebook, Instagram and Twitter accounts for anything that would lead them to their first victim, which was America Duvall. After reviewing America's media pages, listening closely to her lyrics, and seeing her with Jay Z, they believed a slip up from her would lead to a huge payday.

After doing a background check, they found out where she lived, and when they saw her car pulling out of her estate's driveway, they followed her. But, the only thing was, the person behind the tinted windows of the luxury vehicle listed in America's name was Ren, and not her. The two detectives didn't realize that until they saw Ren get out of the C-Class coupe.

"Who the fuck is that?" Detective Gordy asked her partner.

"I don't know. The more important question is, what's in the bag he's carrying," Detective Burnam replied.

"Looks empty."

"Hm, he's here to fill it up. I wonder who's behind the motel door," Detective Gordy said with her hand on the car door lever.

"Hold up, let's wait till he gets in there, then we'll kick the door in. It gives us probable cause to search the room. That way, we don't need a warrant, and killin' muthafuckas is justifiable," Detective Burnam said, holding his partner back.

"You're right. All we gotta say is that we were following a lead, and when we saw the suspect kick the door in, we protected and served."

****

Inside room 106 of the Pittsburgh Inn, Smack Down stood talking to JB.

Smack Down said, "This idiot pulls up in a fuckin' C-Class to pick up five ki's. What the fuck!". He was looking out of the motel room window, talking to JB on his burner cell phone.

"Looks like he brought company with him, too, Smack," JB said.

"You bullshittin'! Dumb muthafucka." Smack Down couldn't believe that Ren had brought the police to him.

"He's about to knock on the door," JB told Smack Down. *Knock! Knock! Knock!*

Smack Down killed the lights, and opened the door for Ren. "Get in here! You brought the fuckin' cops with you!" Smack Down said to Ren through clenched teeth.

"What? I ain't bring no po-po wit' me!"

"Shut the fuck up, and help me move these joints to the other room," Smack Down instructed. He had an adjoining room. *Fuckin' po-po! Who even talks like that anymore?* he thought to himself, picking up four of the kilos.

"Grab that one," he told Ren, holding his cell phone to his ear with his shoulder.

"They're comin' to the door. Get the fuck outta there, Smack!" JB told Smack Down.

"They're comin'. Hurry up!" Smack Down said to Ren, mouthing it more than saying it out loud. He didn't want the police to hear his voice.

Ren grabbed the fifth kilo up, and tried to make it to the adjoining room, but it was too late.

Detective Burnam kicked the motel room door in. "Get down! Get on the floor! Get on the floor!" Ren did as he was told.

Detective Gordy turned on the lights. Ren looked at the closed door that would have led to his escape, and went down to the floor. Hearing the police kick the door in, Smack Down closed and locked it.

Outside, JB waited for the detectives to enter the motel room, and drove slowly up to the room Smack Down was in. "Come on, Smack. I'm out front, you good," JB said.

Smack Down ran out of the room and jumped into JB's car with an overnight bag with four ki's in it.

"Nigga, you crazy. You should've left that shit," JB said, pulling off fast.

"Yea, right! I wasn't leavin' shit! That stupid muthafucka's loss is now my gain," Smack Down said, looking in back of him through the passenger side mirror, making sure they were not being followed.

Meanwhile, back at the club, Sexy Duvall walked inside of Dominican Flames' office to meet with both America and Dominican Flames. Sexy Duvall asked, looking at America and Dominican Flames, "Y'all good now?" They had just ended their conference call with Dominican Flames' father, Brooklyn Pete, from a cell at USP Cannan.

"Yea, we good," America said, wiping tears from her eyes. "Yea, ma, we straight," Dominican Flames said, extending her arms to hug America.

"I'm sorry, sis," America said, hugging Dominican Flames, and just like that, their beef was dead.

"Love you, A."

"Love you, too, Dom."

Sexy Duvall watched the two of them as joy filled

her heart. The thought of her losing one of them because of video footage of her shooting brought tears to her eyes. She loved the two of them that much. Losing her mother was hard enough.

Brooklyn Pete had said some harsh words to both of them. He was hard on them, but he spoke the truth.

"So, now, let's get back to this money, bitches," Sexy Duvall said, making all of them laugh.

“Yea, Smack?" America said, answering her ringing phone.

"Ya dumb ass brotha got busted! He brought the fuckin' police to me!" Smack Down yelled into the phone.

"Hol' up, what? What you mean? Where? Where the fuck is he, Smack? Where? Okay, I'm on my way over there," America said, and the call disconnected.

"What happened, A?" Sexy Duvall asked.

“Yea, what the fuck's up, sis?" Dominican Flames asked.

"Ren got busted at a motel on 65," America said, sitting down, putting her face in her hands.

"I told you 'bout that nigga," Sexy Duvall said, talking about Smack Down.

"Shut up, Ma! It wasn't his fault! Ren was being followed, and led the cops to the pick-up spot," America said.

"How the fuck he get away and my son didn't?"

"Ma, I don't know!"

"I keep tellin' his ass he ain't no hustla. You goin' in to ya stash to get him out 'cause I ain't payin' fo' that shit!"

"Ma, I ain't ask you to. I got this!"

"I'll help you get his fine ass out, but he gotta do house arrest at my spot," Dominican Flames said light heartedly.

America and her mother laughed.

****

BACK AT THE PITTSBURGH INN

"I know what'cha thinkin'. I'm done, I'm not sayin' shit. How the fuck am I goin' to get outta this shit? But we don't want to put you in jail. We not tryna take ya product and flip it. What the fuck do we want then? Well, here's ya answer: we want fifty Gs, and you can go. You could prolly make that off the kilo sittin' beside you."

Ren looked down at the brick sitting next to him, and then looked back up at the dirty detectives.

"But, unless you get that fifty Gs within the next hour, you'll never get to sell that bitch," Detective Burnam continued saying.

"I can get that. Hand me my phone," Ren said.

"You'll get ya chance to pay up, but first, we're goin' to call Mr. Bucks. We're gon' let him pay us, and you can pay him back. You may not get it, but we're tryna impress the man and let him know how important it is for him to keep us around. I know the show y'all doin' is a rap show, but we got ways to turn all you muthafuckas into singers," Detective Gordy said.

"Man, let me get y'all this money so I can get outta this bitch. Leave the show out of it; I ain't got no part in that shit," Ren said.

"You're not, but America Duvall is. Who is she, ya sister? Looking at ya ID, I see you have the same address and last name," Detective Burnam said.

"Yea, she's my sister. Look, I'll give y'all a hunnid racks if y'all leave her out of this," Ren said.

"You hear that, partner? The price for him just went up fifty thousand," Detective Gordy said.

"This is bullshit!" Ren responded.

"Nah, this is real shit!" Detective Burnam said. "See, ya not gettin' the big picture. It's not about you; it's about us establishing a new arrangement with Mr. Bucks. Give him a call, partner, and let him know the current situation," Detective Burnam said.

****

IN SAN FRANCISCO

Monte Bucks and Money King were leaving Tadich Grill. "I can't believe we flew all the way to San Francisco so you could eat here," Money said as she was elevated out of her wheelchair and into the Blue/Moccasin Tan interior back seat of a midnight sapphire blue seashell Rolls-Royce Phantom.

"What can I say, baby? I love spicy Cioppino," Monte Bucks said to Money as he also climbed into the back seat from the opposite side.

Cioppino was a tomato-wine stew, brimming with clams, mussels, shrimp, whitefish, and Dungeness crab. It came with a few slices of butter-soaked garlic bread made from Boudin sourdough, and was prepared by chef Wil Going.

"But Wil just opened another Tadich Grill in D.C. We could have flown there instead of flying all the way to San Fran, Monte," Money said, trying figure out the riddle in her head.

"Okay, you busted me. I wanted as much time alone with you as I could get. Matter of fact, I want to spend the night with you and tomorrow before we fly home to Pittsburgh. We can stop and eat Szechuan shrimp and Mao Po Tofu specially prepared by our chef friend, Susanna Foo in Philadelphia."

Money let what Monte was saying sink in, then his cell phone rang. Money watched as he studied the caller's name on his screen.

"It's those pesky, money hungry cops again. Set ya phone to record this call. I really don't trust these muthafuckas. We need something to use against these muthafuckas whenever they decide to get outta hand," Monte Bucks told Money.

"Ready," Money said, pressing record on her cell phone.

"Yes, what do you have for me this time?" Monte

Bucks asked Detective Burnam.

"We got one of ya guys, Renault Duvall, and a kilogram of pure, white cocaine."

"Renault Duvall, that's not one of my guys. He's not on the show," Monte Bucks said, looking over at Money to see if he was missing anything.

"That's Sexy's son. He's the one we got fighting Dominica's men," Money said in a whisper.

"Yea, yea, yea, I know he's not on the show, but he's the brother of one of the main characters on the show, you know, America Duvall?"

"All right, so why'd you call me?"

"Well, I'm calling because I don't want the show catching any more heat before the season starts. You're already two murders and a shooting in, and now a kilogram of cocaine. All that, plus a successful show, sounds like a racketeering case waiting to happen. And we, me and my partner, don't want you going through the hassle of an investigation, Mr. Bucks because me and my partner, Detective Gordy, love what you're doing for these kids in our city, don't we, Gordy?"

"Yes, we do. It's great," Detective Gordy replied.

Monte Bucks and Money King looked at each other, shaking their heads. "So, what do you suggest I do?" Monte Bucks asked.

"You pay us a hundred grand, and we make this go away. I'm pretty sure this guy will pay you back."

"You got it. I'll have my people call you within the hour."

"Thank you, Mr. Bucks. Nice doin' business with you," Detective Burnam said, looking at Detective Gordy with a smile on his face. Their plan had worked.

"Hey, can I speak to Renault?" Monte Bucks asked.

"Sure," Detective Burnam handed his phone over to Ren, but before he could say a word, Money grabbed Monte Bucks' phone and hung it up.

"We don't need you talking to him," she told Monte Bucks.

"Yea?" Ren said into the dead phone line. "The call must've dropped," Ren said before handing Detective Burnam his phone back.

"Well, it's ya lucky day. But hey, do me a favor and let us bust ya ass again. That was the easiest hundred grand we've ever made," Detective Burnam said before he and his partner walked out of the motel room.

"Hope you gotta couple extra bucks. They're gonna want you to pay fo' this, and you better take care of it," Detective Gordy said, pointing at the crashed door.

After Monte Bucks spoke to Detective Burnam, Money King called Sexy Duvall. The phone rang twice before Sexy Duvall answered. "Yea, Money. Sis, what's up?"

"Hi, babe." Money's voice cut through the muffled sound of music playing in the background. America and Dominican Flames had left to find Ren on 65, but she had stayed at the club due to her injuries.

"I got some good and bad news," Money continued.

"I know what the bad news is; Ren got picked up. So, what's the good news?" Sexy Duvall asked.

"The cops who arrested him, let him go. We took care of it. It cost us a hunnid stacks, but it's as if it never happened."

"Thanks, sis. I'll pay you back. Don't worry 'bout that." "That's the least of my worries. Do me a favor, tho'. Make sure he leaves the drugs alone. The police mentioned a racketeering charge. They're going to be watching us for a while tryna find shit to hold over our heads. We don't need that, you know?"

"I feel you, and I'ma make sure he does. That muthafucka ain't no street nigga. Trust me, I got his ass."

"Okay, thanks."

"Thank you! Love you, sis, and tell Monte I said thanks."

"Love you too. Will do," Money King replied before hanging up.

"That nigga set me up!" Ren told America and Dominican Flames, leaving the cheap motel on 65. Dominican Flames had one of her men take Ren's car and the kilo of cocaine to a safe place.

"Ren, what are you talkin' about? Why would he do that?" America asked, defending Smack Down.

"I know he did. That shit was too shady. That nigga was on his phone the whole time. He was talking to the cops the whole time," Ren said hysterically.

At the same time, America's phone vibrated. "Yea, Ma. Okay. Here, bro," America said, handing Ren her cell phone.

"Ma, that muthafucka set me up! I'ma deal wit' that nigga!" Ren screamed into the phone.

"Ya ass ain't doin' shit! Ya not gon' fuck our money up reactin' to ya silly-ass theory! I've known that man for years. Snitchin' ain't his M.O. See, ya ass is gon' get us cut from the show, and I ain't havin' that shit," Sexy Duvall said, screaming. She calmed down, and tried to talk sense into her son. "Now, where are you?"

"We're on our way to the club."

"A'ight, I'll see you when you get here. Promise me ya not gonna do nothin' stupid."

"I promise," Ren said before hanging up with his mother.

Listening to her brother and mother talk, America thought about what her brother was saying. Even though she knew Smack Down would never set her brother up, she still analyzed what he was saying, trying to see the logic in it, but there was none. Shaking her head, she shook the thought of Smack Down's betrayal.

Thinking about the anger she heard in his voice, she scrolled through her call log and pressed Smack Down's number. "This number has been changed or is no longer in service," the recording echoed in her ear. *What the fuck?* she thought, wondering if she had just lost five hundred thousand dollars.

CHAPTER 20:

PURPLE ONE STILL REIGNS

The next morning, Monte Bucks' Falcon 7x flew from San Francisco to Philadelphia as he and Money watched an episode of Billionaire. "Have you ever used these?" Monte Bucks asked, picking up a pair of LG 360 VR Glasses.

"Nope, not yet," Money replied.

"You gotta check 'em out, they're incredible. I need to come up with something like this," Monte Bucks said as his cell phone rang. "See who that is for me, babe," he said. His cell phone was closer to Money.

"It says Tyka," Money said.

"Tyka, that's Prince's sister. Let me see," Money pressed answer, and handed Monte Bucks his phone. "Tyka? What's up, baby girl?" Monte answered, but there was silence. "Tyka?" he said again, this time looking at the screen of his phone.

"He's gone, Monte," Tyka said in a low, dispirited voice.

"What you mean? Who's gone? What are you talkin' about, Tyka?" Monte asked with worry in his voice. He felt weak, and took a seat on the edge of Money's recliner. He listened for a response.

Days before this call, Prince had called him and told him that he had an emergency landing in Moline, Illinois on the way home after doing a show, April 14th, but decided to leave after the hospital could not compliment his stay. That night, he had performed two shows, and did three encores.

Two days after that, April 16th, Prince had called him and invited him to a show he was having at Paisley, but he had told him he was in another country handling business and couldn't make it. It was that night that Prince had eerily told the crowd to "Wait a few days before wasting their prayers on him." So, in Monte Bucks' mind, Tyka could not possibly be talking about her brother.

"Prince. My brother's dead, Monte."

"What do you mean he's dead? I just talked to him. NO! NO! Don't tell me no shit like that, Tyka! Is this some type of joke?" Monte's voice trembled. He didn't know how to respond to the heart-stopping news. Tears poured from his eyes and his heart ached with grief.

Money rubbed his back. She couldn't hear what Tyka was saying, but she knew that he could only be talking about the Purple One they had all known as Prince.

Money had only met Prince once at one of his charity events, but had known him all her life through his music. Slowly, she lost control of her upper lip, and her nose burned as she began to cry also. Sadness had overcome the both of them.

"We found him unresponsive on an elevator at Paisley," Tyka continued to say.

"You're shittin' me, Tyka."

“No, Monte, I wish I were. Hey, the police are on

my other line. I gotta call you back."

"Tyka, please keep me posted. I'm on my way there," Monte said. "What about the funeral? What do you need me to do?"

"He didn't want a funeral, Monte. We're going to have a private cremation service in a few days. I will keep you posted so you can attend. I know how close the two of you were. He loved you like a brother. I gotta go, but like I said, I'll keep you posted. Love ya."

"Love you, too. I'm sorry, sis. Truly I am," Monte said. "Talk to you soon, brother," Tyka said before clicking over to her other line.

Hearing how much Prince loved him really tore Monte Bucks up inside. Hundreds of people had seen him perform for the last time, had even seen his friend and brother do three encores, but because of business, he wasn't there. "I wasn't there. I WASN'T THERE!" Monte Bucks said, rocking back and forth. "He called me and told me

to come see him perform, not once but twice. I missed him both times. He knew Jehovah was calling him home. Him and God were close, you know? God was in all his songs. He's in a place he wants to be, at Jehovah's side," Monte Bucks said. Money just listened to him, wiping tears from her eyes.

"Where's the remote, babe?" Monte asked.

"Right here."

"Turn on CNN."

"The Breaking News has been confirmed. Music icon, Prince, dead at age 57..."

"Oooh... Oh my God, Prince. PRRRINNNCE!" Monte wailed, falling back onto Money. She held her new man with tears flooding from her eyes.

The night before, they had decided to be a couple. She had grown tired of Smack Down, and his crooked street ways. Him leaving her dinner to handle his street business was the final straw. Now something had happened that would bond her and her new man for life.

"This can't be real. It feels like a nightmare, Money. I just talked to him and he was mad that I couldn't make it to his last show, but we were out of the country."

"I know, baby. He forgives you," Money said, comforting Monte Bucks.

"You want to hear my favorite song by him?"

"Yes, baby. What is it?" Money asked as Monte searched his phone for the song he loved the most by Prince.

"'Everybody Loves Purple Rain', 'When Doves Cry' and Let's Go Crazy. My favorite songs is 'Sometimes It Snows In April'." Monte pressed play on his phone, and the song began to play. The guitar and piano played slowly. The song was about a friend named Tracy. A friend who had died in a war. It spoke of death and love, and the snow that sometimes fell in April. *"Always cry for love, never cry for pain,"* said the lyrics. *"I'm not afraid to die,"* Prince sung.

"Baby, I have an idea. Why don't we have a party in memory of Prince? Let's have Dominica do her club all purple, play all of Prince's songs and movies, and represent him like it's 1999!"

"YES! That's a great idea," Monte sat up and said. "I want to invite everybody. Call Jimmy Jam and Terry Lewis, Morris and the Time, Lenny Waronker. Let's get D'Angelo to perform," Monte Bucks said, and kissed Money. "What are you waiting for, baby? Call Dominica. Tell her we're celebrating Prince's death tonight."

"I'm on it," Money said, going through her call log for Dominican Flames' number. She smiled, happy to see that her idea had brought joy back into Monte Bucks' heart as well as hers.

****

Back in Pittsburgh, things weren't as joyous for Blocks N Bricks. His home had been raided earlier that morning, and he had been served an indictment. Now, he was sitting in a cold cell in federal holding, waiting to make his first appearance.

"Ain't this you?" one of the federal agents came pass his cell and asked, showing him a picture of him and Rick Ross posing at the teaser party in the Hip Hop Weekly LTMP Special Edition.

Blocks N Bricks looked at himself in the picture, but didn't say a word. In the cell beside him, he could hear his homies talking about the indictment, but he just sat back and listened to them. He wasn't in the mood to talk. The more of them that came into the holding area, the sicker he felt. My rap career's over, he thought.

CHAPTER 21:

PARTY LIKE IT'S 1999

That night at Reflection Night Club, fans of Prince poured into the doors. Monte Bucks had even called in a favor from the Mayor of Pittsburgh. He had gotten a permit, and was allowed to set up huge monitors outside of the club, along with huge movie screens to display the movie *Purple Rain*, and play Prince's music all night long.

Inside of the club, it was packed with fans, the LTMP cast, and celebrities. Making his way to the V.I.P. section, Smack Down was stopped by Ren. "I know you set me up, nigga," Ren told Smack Down, grabbing him by his arm.

"Whatever, nigga! Get the fuck off me! Ain't nobody set'cha dumb ass up!" Smack Down said, pulling away from Ren.

"SMACK!" America ran up to Smack Down with open arms and hugged him. As she did so, Ren and Smack Down locked eyes, but there was someone else keeping their eyes on Smack Down as well. Money was watching him from her V.I.P. booth.

"Everybody, let me get your attention," Monte Bucks said, speaking into the mic at the DJ booth. Everybody in the club listened to what he was about to say. "Dearly beloved, we are gathered here today to get through this thing called life. Electric word life, it means forever, and that's a mighty long time. But I'm here to tell you that there's something else, the after world..." Everybody in the club recited Prince's lyrics with Monte

Bucks. The DJ stopped the music at Monte's cue. "Prince was a close friend of mine. I met him during my first tour, and we remained friends for close to thirty years. I loved him as a brother, and I know everybody in here loves him."

"Yaaaay!" the crowd went crazy.

"Tonight! We gon' represent Prince like it's nineteen..." "Ninety-nine!" the crowd completed the lyric.

"DJ Schizo, let's represent, baby!"

"Yay!" The crowd went crazy again.

Prince's guitar let out a mean riff. Prince wailed a few exotic moans, the piano played a few keys, the beat was melodic, then he started to sing.

"Dig if you will the picture,

you and I engaged in a kiss,

the sweat of the body covers me" Prince's "When Doves Cry" played, and everybody inside and outside of the club sang along.

Monte Bucks held a bottle of champagne up to Money King, and she held her champagne flute up to him from her V.I.P. booth.

America and Dominican Flames danced as Sexy Duvall watched in their V.I.P. booth.

Smack Down and JB held up their baller bottles while Ren and C.O. Hooker watched them.

Prince had brought them all together, and for that night, all beefs and business was on hold while Blocks N

Bricks and his co-dee's sat in a federal correctional facility in Ohio, being processed.

****

When 7:46 a.m. arrived, Monte Bucks found himself at Bucks Plaza Hotel. He watched CNN as they spoke about his late friend, Prince. The camera crew from the *Today* show had just packed up and exited his boardroom. He waited for the cast members of LTMP to arrive. They were having a mandatory meeting. Monte Bucks wanted to discuss something with them and show the rough edit of episode one.

Around 7:51 A.M., the cast members started arriving; America and Sexy Duvall, DQ Dawg, Dominican Flames, Boom Bap, Mr. Frosty Blow, Smack Down and finally, Making Hitz. There were two empty seats at the table; one was Money King's, she rarely attended the board meetings, and the other was Blocks N Bricks.

"While we were mourning Prince and partying last night, Blocks N Bricks and his crew were getting indicted and processed. I put a folder in front of all of you. I want y'all to study the faces of the two individuals pictured in the folder," Monte Bucks said as he watched everyone look at the photographs of Detectives Burnam and Gordy.

"They're tryna shut us down, but we can't let that happen. But, the way shit's been lately—murder, drugs, shootings—we're headed that way before we even get started, and they reminded me of that recently. I can't let that happen, so if I have to start cuttin' fingers off to save my hand, I will. Straighten y'all's shit up," Monte Bucks said, studying his group of cast members. "I'ma do what I can for Blocks N Bricks, and whatever for the rest of the family, but don't play me! Don't have me involved with no federal shit. I don't need to do this. I'm doin' this for y'all. I'm doin' this for our city, so use me, but don't abuse me," Monte Bucks continued, picking up a remote for the huge TV monitor in the boardroom.

“Now we're about to look at the rough cut of episode one. I'm looking for some feedback. If we need to tighten shit up, let me know. We want our shit the tightest," Monte Bucks told his cast members as he leaned back in his seat and pressed play on the remote.

"This is season one of *Love & Trap Muzik, Pittsburgh*!"

DO YOU HAVE WHAT IT TAKES TO BE AN AUTHOR? NEW OR OLD...

Made in the USA
Monee, IL
01 October 2024